Native American Literature: A Very Short Introduction

VERY SHORT INTRODUCTIONS are for anyone wanting a stimulating
and accessible way into a new subject. They are written by experts, and
have been translated into more than 45 different languages.

The series began in 1995, and now covers a wide variety of topics in
every discipline. The VSI library now contains over 500 volumes—a Very
Short Introduction to everything from Psychology and Philosophy of
Science to American History and Relativity—and continues to grow in every
subject area.

Very Short Introductions available now:

Sean Teuton

NATIVE AMERICAN LITERATURE

A Very Short Introduction

OXFORD
UNIVERSITY PRESS

OXFORD
UNIVERSITY PRESS

Oxford University Press is a department of the University of Oxford.
It furthers the University's objective of excellence in research, scholarship,
and education by publishing worldwide. Oxford is a registered trademark of
Oxford University Press in the UK and certain other countries.

Published in the United States of America by Oxford University Press
198 Madison Avenue, New York, NY 10016, United States of America.

Library of Congress Cataloging-in-Publication Data
Names: Teuton, Sean Kicummah, 1966- author.
Title: Native American literature : a very short introduction / Sean Teuton.
Description: New York : Oxford University Press, 2018. | Series: Very short
introductions | Includes bibliographical references and index.
Identifiers: LCCN 2017021510 (print) | LCCN 2017021702 (ebook) |
ISBN 9780199944538 (updf) | ISBN 9780199944545 (epub) |
ISBN 9780190231392 (online product) |
ISBN 9780199944521 (paperback : acid-free paper)
Subjects: LCSH: American literature—Indian authors—History and criticism. |
Indians in literature.
Classification: LCC PS153.I52 (ebook) | LCC PS153.I52 T465 2018 (print) |
DDC 810.9/897—dc23
LC record available at https://lccn.loc.gov/2017021510

1 3 5 7 9 8 6 4 2

Printed in Great Britain
by Ashford Colour Press Ltd., Gosport, Hants.
on acid-free paper

For Xavier

Contents

List of illustrations

Native American Literature

Preface

"Don't any of you kill him, he is a different kind of man, let's look him over." This was the testimony of some Native American hunters on their discovery of a European explorer. Literature lets us, like curious hunters, imagine other lives. In reading we enter a world where actual people or characters relate experiences perhaps extremely different from our own. Through that process, we may come to understand or even share some of the views or values of another. In literature is thus the power to transform. Native American literature offers that transformation to its readers—but also represents it in its pages. Whether through an ancient epic on diplomacy, an antebellum public address on Native rights, or a contemporary novel about human interaction with animals, Native literature displays a dynamic world inextricably connected to and even fascinated with other worlds. After all, long before Europeans arrived in North America indigenous peoples were neither timeless nor culturally pure. Instead for centuries, distinct Native nations interacted and transformed each other, often in response to their changing world. They adapted. When Europeans first visited, primarily to conquer and to plunder, they nonetheless entered a vast, codified network of trade not only in goods but also in ideas. Today, after more than 500 years of exchange, Native American literature both struggles and thrives at a crossroads of conflict and cooperation.

This volume relies on that truth about interaction and adaptation—from Native origins, through the European conquest and cultural destruction, and into the recovery and revitalization of indigenous communities today. Throughout their journey, Native American authors spoke or wrote not only to defend and to inspire their nations, but also in wonder for other worlds and peoples, and to reach them.

Chapter 1
The man made of words

It was March 1970. The previous July the United States had put a man on the moon, in May the Beatles would release the album *Let It Be*, and Native Americans occupied Alcatraz Island in San Francisco Bay to raise hell about the poverty on reservations. At Princeton University the Kiowa writer N. Scott Momaday addressed the First Convocation of American Indian Scholars: "We are," he said, "what we imagine. Our very existence consists in our imagination of ourselves. Our best destiny is to imagine...who and what, and *that* we are."

Momaday knew that Native people had to reimagine themselves were they ever to recover from the nearly 500 years of conquest and disease that devastated indigenous peoples in North America. Government policies designed to eradicate indigenous cultures also worked to convince Native Americans themselves that they must surrender their traditional lives to survive as North American moderns. Either way, so went the American story, Indians were destined to disappear. Defiantly, Momaday and others extolled the imagination's power to reclaim a freed vision of indigenous history, community, land, and knowledge. The liberation from that American story of Indian demise, Momaday urges, must begin in the mind. In this defining moment, Native people took possession of their own lives to envision a future of pride and flourishing. They would revisit their history and reimagine another destiny, says Momaday, through story, through literature: "Man tells stories in order to understand his experience…[and] achieves the fullest realization of his humanity in…literature." For Native Americans this model of literature promises nothing less than the retention and future of indigenous worldviews. As Momaday and others of his day well knew, it would be no small feat to imagine a literature to serve a Native American movement. And yet they did it.

In 1968 Momaday published his first novel, *House Made of Dawn*, about a combat veteran in World War II named Abel who suffers a beating at the hands of racist police in Los Angeles, then returns to his New Mexico pueblo to retrace his relationship to his culture and land, and finally achieves wholeness and belonging. The novel ends with great hope for Native people. Readers have come to share in Abel's struggle to regain his spiritual and bodily health when he wakes, runs, and sings in a ceremonial race: "[Abel] ran on…and under his breath he began to sing ….*House made of pollen, house made of dawn*."

Momaday's novel won the Pulitzer Prize for fiction in 1969, but, more importantly, it sparked an unabated explosion of Native American novel, short story, poetry, autobiography, and drama. Today Louise Erdrich, James Welch, Leslie Silko, Joy Harjo, Sherman Alexie, and Lee Maracle have become household names, and other Native writers abound: The Anishinaabe writer Gerald Vizenor imagines Columbus a descendent of Mayans and Jews who wished to return home to America. David Treuer, who is Ojibwe, sets Native American crime dramas in mid-century Minneapolis. Choctaw author LeAnne Howe's characters investigate an eighteenth-century indigenous sacrifice that calls on the living present. Joseph Boyden, an Anishinaabe novelist, leads Native snipers into the trenches of World War I. Native American literature bears the same complexity and diversity as that found in any body of great literature.

As Native American authors learned to write in English they also mastered literary forms like the novel, adapting these genres to serve indigenous worldviews. Native writers still experiment with language in a way that incorporates oral literatures that have long connected indigenous nations with ancestors and lands, and shaped their communal identities as distinct peoples. Since the Native American literary movement of the 1970s almost all Native literature honors "The Man Made of Words," Momaday's call for imagination and for indigenous oral literatures to celebrate it.

Native Americans have long possessed practical writing systems such as wampum belts and petroglyphs, birch bark scrolls and bison hides, which often serve as mnemonic devices for oral narratives. Such narratives, often accompanied with song and music, dance and drama, describe origins, migrations, social customs, legal obligations, religious values, and ethical responsibilities. Other stories simply entertain, often humorously, by affirming the inherent folly, mystery, and awe of life on earth. Each generation holds the fate of oral literature in its hands; taken lightly or forgotten the stories and the knowledge they convey could be lost.

Historically North American scholars often saw this verbal art as proof of the Indian's primitive state rather than as evidence of indigenous literary imagination. Though the pilgrims sailed to America in 1620 on the promise to convert Indians to Christianity and away from their orally transmitted beliefs, once Native Americans gained alphabetic literacy in English they began to express their oral literature in written form. By the 1660s Native people attended Harvard and learned Latin and Greek, and by 1720 missionary Eleazor Wheelock's Mohegan students Samson Occom and Joseph Johnson, and Hendrick Aupaumut, who was Mahican, produced some of the first Native American autobiographies and sermons in English.

Not until the 1820s, however, did Native Americans take control of English literacy to combat racism, build indigenous nations, and retain lands. Around this time a nonliterate Cherokee silversmith named Sequoyah invented North America's first indigenous alphabet. In a matter of weeks Cherokees began creating their own literature without the aid of English. In 1828 Elias Boudinot, John Ridge, and John Ross helped establish the first Native American newspaper, the *Cherokee Phoenix*, in English and in Cherokee, in which they recorded traditions, reported or opposed federal Indian policy, and put Native people in touch with the global world. Also around this time Pequot minister William Apess began to preach throughout New England to Europeans, Natives, and Africans alike, and he wrote in defense of those he presciently termed people "of color." Others such as Seneca activist Maris Bryant Pierce and Cherokee missionary student Catherine Brown composed national histories and conversion narratives.

In this era Native Americans adapted mostly nonfiction forms to serve specific political needs. As they protected or even suppressed their oral literatures and advanced their western learning to promote diplomacy, Native writers composed histories and essays, addresses and editorials. Out west where, by the middle nineteenth century, the reach of the North American empire remained tenuous, indigenous people began to collaborate with translators and amanuenses to compose numerous autobiographies. While ethnologists perhaps saw the goal of this work as the preservation of a dying way of life, Native Americans sought to tell the world *their* story of America. Recorders gained the accounts of famous warriors such as Black Hawk and Geronimo, often at the expense of Native women's personal narratives. Nonetheless, in the autobiographical genre we see the first emphatic emergence of indigenous women's voices, and some women describe their experiences as medicine makers and healers, war leaders and diplomats. Crow wise woman Pretty Shield details a prophecy from her "ant helpers" entirely in Indian sign language, while Paiute lecturer Sarah Winnemucca scouts for the U.S. cavalry and carries a knife in her stocking. Well into the twentieth century the autobiographies of such Sioux authors as Charles Eastman and Luther Standing Bear offer pre-contact experience and subsequent mastery of westernization as a critique of North American society.

The Cherokee journalist John Rollin Ridge published the first Native novel, *Joaquin Murieta*, in 1854, and the first novel by a Native American woman, Creek Alice Callahan's *Wynema*, appeared in 1891. Despite these firsts, creative work in fiction, poetry, and drama did not mature until the 1930s, when, after decades of federal policy set on destroying indigenous culture, Native populations and vitality had seen their nadir. Perhaps for this reason Native American writers turned in earnest to fiction for the first time; here they could harness the imaginative wonder preserved in oral literature to revive and sustain indigenous communities. Such would explain the defeatism also at play in the era's novels, such as in Osage writer John Joseph Mathews's *Sundown* (1934) and Salish intellectual D'Arcy McNickle's *Surrounded* (1936). By the explosive 1960s, however, Native writers such as Momaday would imagine a new Native American literature, one in touch with oral literature, to write new endings *as* new beginnings for Native people.

A different American story

Narrative serves to explain the world, especially when that world faces crisis: a Keresan creation story describes the arrival of some of the first deities in the form of twins. One remained but the other traveled east to reside beyond a great body of water, promising one day to return and reunite with his twin. The prophecies of other Native nations predict the arrival of long-lost relatives from other shores. Such stories no doubt helped indigenous peoples understand the arrival of Europeans. In view of such prophecies, Native people may have thought that European invaders arriving on horseback and covered in armor were gods. But if so this deification was short-lived, and it underscores the fact that indigenous peoples possessed their own literatures long before the arrival of Europeans.

Of course before the coming of Columbus, the peoples indigenous to the Americas did not call themselves "Indians," as the admiral wrongly dubbed them. In fact they probably had no shared identity that spanned the hemispheres or even North America. Instead, these small groups often called themselves by names roughly translating as "The People." Each of these peoples shared a commonly held land, language, kinship, and belief about their place in the universe. Aside from these similarities, indigenous peoples in North America differ greatly. As a people adapted to a particular region, they developed subsistence patterns and belief systems tied deeply to that specific land.

While some Native Americans have oral histories of migrations, others explain their creation as a literal emergence from a sacred landscape. On the southern planes Kiowas tell of crawling from a hollow log; in the northeastern woodlands Mohawks describe falling through a hole in the sky to land on a turtle floating on the water. Paleoanthropologists have developed theories of great migrations of Paleolithic people from Asia to the Americas as early as 75,000 years ago. Around that time giant glaciers covered much of North America, causing sea levels to drop and exposing land in the Bering Strait. Pleistocene animals, megafauna such as giant bison and wooly mammoths grazed across this land bridge, and hunters followed. The hunters probably made their way down the west coast, all the way to the tip of South America. More and more experts believe that Native Americans also arrived by sea, as maritime traders across the Pacific Ocean. Today some Native leaders and scholars question the Land Bridge theory, claiming that it conveniently suggests that Indians too are actually settlers.

Around 200 BCE increasing agriculture began to spur larger settlements across North America, especially in the Ohio Valley. Excavators in the nineteenth century named their founders the

6

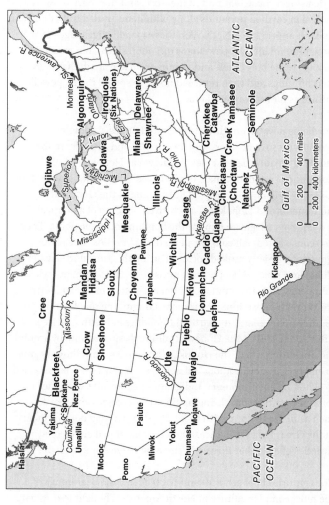

1. Native American nations in their ancestral homes, c. 1500 CE

Hopewellians. They built enormous, geometric earthworks, embankments, circles, and squares more than a thousand feet wide using a consistent unit of measure, and they buried revered leaders in earthen pyramids along with items traded from distant lands. It appears that Native Americans made pilgrimages to these monuments; Hopewellians did not reside in but seemed to manage these holy cities, and visitors from afar might have left their offerings and then returned home to spread the Hopewell culture as far as North Dakota.

In what is now the southwestern United States, a complex agricultural society emerged between 900 and 1500 CE. In the southern Arizona desert a people known as Hohokams built a stone-lined system of canals to divert water from the Gila and Salt Rivers to irrigate their crops. The building of the Hopewell monuments and Hohokam canals gives evidence of a political system, even a legal system for the handling of water rights. They also constructed ball courts and earthen pyramids to serve an apparently strictly ranked society. During this time northeast of Hohokam, Anasazi people built massive brick apartment-style complexes that still stand today. Pueblo Bonito in Chaco Canyon has more than two hundred rooms and until the nineteenth century was the largest apartment building in North America. After about 400 CE the Hopewell culture dissipated and, by around the fifteenth century, the Hohokam and Anasazi dwellings began to empty. These civilizations did not mysteriously vanish but adapted to changing environments. Indigenous people left these cities to form new settlements, bringing their technologies and new foods, such as maize or corn, with them. By 800 CE indigenous farmers in the Great Lakes, Northeast, and Southeast had engineered varieties of corn that thrived in their own region and climate.

The centuries between 800 and 1000 CE saw the beginnings of the most complex culture in North America. Thought to originate in the Mississippi River valley, Mississippians distributed their religious complex far into the Southeast and into Oklahoma, with at least one population center that remained into the eighteenth century. They designed cities and built platform mounds, plazas, and defensive walls with bastions. Just east of St. Louis lies the empty city of Cahokia, where as many as 20,000 Native Americans lived and prospered before the largest earthen pyramid in North America, at more than 100 feet high.

Archaeologists find that Mississippians participated in ranked societies ruled by hereditary priests. To honor these rulers, commoners and outlying chiefdoms paid tribute, sometimes even in sacrifice. A labor division enabled the creation of an elaborate material culture. Mass food production, mostly in corn, was needed to feed the temple builders, and so hunters and farmers worked harder to satisfy this demand, establishing colonies as far away as Wisconsin. The ruling class was buried with vast collections of status goods, which were traded far and wide to amass them. Gods of earth and sky, corn mother and bird man, as well as a panoply of spirits, informed their universe and gave meaning and purpose to work, rank, and community belonging, as suggested in Mississippian iconography found on funerary objects. By 1400 CE inhabitants abandoned Cahokia as well as other Mississippian centers, and they likely moved to regions with more resources or more democratic societies.

2. In an artist's reconstruction of the city of Cahokia, c. 1100 CE, as many as 20,000 citizens thrive in a planned, walled city. Athletes compete in the great plaza, while the tallest earthwork north of the Rio Grande stands in the distance.

It remains a matter of debate why indigenous North Americans developed agriculture, since hunting and gathering require less work. We do know that populations increased with the invention of agriculture, but we do not know which came first. Either way, by the time Europeans arrived much of North America relied primarily on planting for subsistence. A few areas rich in hunting resources were the small exceptions: on the Pacific coast thriving salmon peoples had little need for agriculture; Native Americans in the far north and in the Great Basin could not farm their lands but lived primarily by hunting; and on the plains Native groups found vast resources by tracking the annual migrations of bison (or buffalo). Formerly sedentary and practicing agriculture, the buffalo people hunted on the Great Plains in a reversal of nineteenth-century European theories of human civilization that evolves from nomadic hunting to sedentary agriculture. Ironically this cultural exception on the plains came for many North Americans to stand for all Native people. Instead, by 1500 CE indigenous North America was almost entirely agricultural. The Southwest and anywhere east of the Mississippi River saw vast planting and harvesting of corn, beans, and squash—foods known to the Iroquois as the Three Sisters. Hunting supplemented diets, but it was from well-established farms that Native Americans primarily fed their people.

Most everywhere except in the Southwest Native women were the sole farmers. Men cleared fields and hauled harvests, but women hoed and dug, planted and pruned the crops. Some scholars surmise that this gendered division of labor began long before the cultivation of plants, when women first gathered the vegetable parts of indigenous diets. Women learned which plants were nutritious or poisonous, which healed or made good baskets or clothes. From birthing and rearing children Native women learned how to find and make medicines and perhaps for this reason many women became healers and spiritual leaders. Indigenous women were thus often viewed as lifegivers and sustainers in the deepest sense. In fact, in some oral literatures women are synonymous with food itself. For Abenakis and Cherokees the first woman gave birth to corn, and for Cherokees the name of the first woman, Selu, is the same as the name for corn. In ceremony Native Americans honored these spiritual relationships to ensure good harvests.

Indigenous societies often carefully organized their labor, lodges, societies, and even dialects by divisions in gender. Men and women often knew very little of each other's activities and lifeways. Scholars debate whether this gendering was complementarily or disproportionately empowered, but since dualism and balance formed such a part of many belief systems, it is possible that women and men worked separately yet fairly to prosper as one. In matrilineal societies—groups that trace their familial descent through the mother—men married into wives' families and lived with them. Anthropologists often refer to families organized by matrilineal descent as clans. Women often owned the homes and their contents, and they managed the land within the clan system. Possessing such social power, in many communities Native American women held a central place in government. Among Iroquois people clan mothers, heads of extended families, acted as key decision makers especially in wartime. The women who gave the young men their lives helped determine whether a situation merited the risking of those lives.

Native men's lives typically concerned warfare and hunting. In each activity men devised complex methods and trained each new generation, often against great danger, to provide for their people. Through rituals honoring the spirits of animals, hunters ensured that migratory game would return and remain plentiful. Boys became men by proving themselves capable hunters and defenders of homelands. Indigenous nations maintained territories, and warfare clarified boundaries that determined group identity with land. While men killed their enemies, war often sought not decimation but displays of national identity, power, and worth. Because war involved also peace agreements with foreign nations, Native American men often engaged in diplomacy and trade.

From the earliest Paleoindigenes who organized to hunt or share work, steadfast social relationships emerged to preserve order and guide moral conduct within a community. Throughout indigenous North America this kinship ensured the very survival of distinct peoples. Indeed, visions of kin responsibilities expanded beyond the human realm to include animals and plants, rocks and weather, and their spirits. At the human level alone complex kin responsibilities varied widely across North America. Within a single Native American group, individual kin could be relatives by biological descent or marriage, or entire groups could share no biological relationship but still consider themselves relatives. In the far north Native people understood themselves to descend both from their mothers and from their fathers, or bilaterally. On the plains among hunting cultures Native Americans tended to define their descent through their fathers. Southwestern and woodland farmers descended through their mothers, a rare phenomenon worldwide.

Kinship likely emerged and endured through the concept of reciprocity since group survival depended on setting aside individual needs for the good of the whole. This system meant that every action in one's daily life in some way must serve the people; one must cooperate on plans, help with work, and share the food. In this manner kinship was also economic. Such kinship obligations were stratified and highly codified, for one belonged not only to a nation, but also to a band, clan, moiety, and various hunting and worship societies, for instance. While social obligations might compete, maintenance of social harmony remained paramount. Group members trusted that others would match their commitment to cooperation and care. Reciprocity was thus demanding and even restrictive on the one hand, but a social safety net on the other.

Kinship also served as a criminal legal system. When one's relative died at the hands of another kin group, one was obligated to kill or adopt one from that group to restore the loss. While this "law of blood" may seem extreme, in the balance much bloodshed was averted. Rather than entire nations going to war over a single accidental death, one person's adoption into the clan network brought lasting peace. As kinship served diplomacy, so it enabled political organization. Certain kin groups rose to power, but kinsmen could challenge this power simply by refusing to follow. Among Natchez people custom demanded that elites marry commoners, one assumes to protect against the consolidation of kin power. To dishonor kinship and its reciprocity with selfishness or arrogance was to self-destruct in isolation or banishment.

The North American indigenous world was alive with unseen spirits that were thought to produce and govern the survival of all life in the universe. And all aspects of the universe were alive, including rocks, thunder, and wind. Even objects such as baskets or pipes could have personhood. Native Americans could gain access to spiritual power through prayer, ritual, and ceremony, and a people's very survival depended on properly meeting these spiritual obligations. Neglect of the spirit world might bring flood or drought, famine or illness. Bountiful agriculture required renewal ceremonies at harvest, and successful hunts demanded prayer and gratitude.

Spiritual leaders mastered oral narratives that reviewed and affirmed the people's sacred covenants with the spirit world, and they led others in dramatic recognition of this through song and dance. Throughout indigenous North America belief systems varied widely. In the Southeast the sacred fire embodied the sun and formed the center of worship, while in the Northeast the longhouse became the vehicle for ceremony. In the Great Lakes region the midewewin medicine society held sway, while on the Pacific coast elaborate dramas commemorated spiritual unions with ancestors. On the Great Plains indigenous groups honored the sundance. Spiritual belief systems, because they were practical, were malleable; indigenous nations borrowed and adapted those ceremonies or rituals they thought applicable and successful.

This was the Native world in North America before the legendary white brothers returned. Coast to coast and from the Arctic Circle to the Rio Grande Native Americans had developed complex and distinct societies that both grew from and drew on particular regions and resources. Though scholarly claims differ, some estimate that five to eight million people inhabited America north of the Rio Grande in 1500, with some four hundred different languages. Indigenous communities handed down their histories and art, government and worship, and even technology. While their machines of war could not match those of Europeans, their ways of healing and medicine might have surpassed them. In today's terms one might say that indigenous economies were often sustainable, and that kinship and worship kept the world alive, mysterious, and satisfying.

Some stubborn myths

On his first voyage to the Americas, Columbus brought beads and bells as gifts to befriend the Arawaks of the Bahamas, but he also brought disease. Because indigenous people raised little livestock, they had virtually no immunity to the contagions brought from the Old World. Evidence shows that Native Americans suffered from arthritis, venereal diseases, and other ailments in pre-contact North America, but nothing as devastating as smallpox and measles, influenza and tuberculosis. A vast network of trade routes throughout the Americas saw the rapid spread of European diseases. Entire communities collapsed, and with them surely entire bodies of knowledge. By 1890 the Native American population in the United States had sunk to 250,000.

Europeans likely knew little about the transmission of disease and its destruction, but of course disease was not the sole cause of

Native decline in North America: warfare and policy played their part too. Whether war or diplomacy carried the day, a relationship between Native Americans and Europeans grew over time, and narrative—literature itself—often stood at the heart of these colonial relations. Europeans held stories about the origin of Native Americans, and Native Americans had their own narratives about the arrival of Europeans. The differing beliefs and values communicated by their narratives informed their ensuing and varying conflictual and cooperative endeavors. Indeed while these narratives across the frontier competed, they as often became entwined, as manifest in hundreds of treaties that bear both European and indigenous signatures.

Spain appealed to the pope by the late fifteenth century for the right to exploit New World resources and peoples, and it justified its conquest with a narrative called the Doctrine of Discovery, which invented the right of Christian royalty to claim dominion over lands of non-Christians still unconquered by other Christian crowns. The Discovery Doctrine also sought to maintain peace between the crowns by precluding the competition for new territories. Mass enslavement, torture, and murder of indigenous people by Spaniards ensued, and by 1550 Bishop Bartolomé de Las Casas debated Juan Ginés de Sepúlveda on whether Native Americans were rational beings capable of voluntary conversion, or whether they were barbarous sinners whom Spain should enslave to forcibly convert. While the conversion of indigenous souls became a mission in the European discovery of the Americas, the conquest of land and its riches drove what some scholars have called the greatest collision of cultures in the history of the world. European invaders continued to justify conquest with powerful legal narratives. By the late sixteenth century France and England sought to join in the plunder of the Americas, and thus sought to modify the Doctrine of Discovery with a new narrative, the Right of Conquest. Dominion, as this new story told it, was not enough to claim territory. A crown must have the might to conquer, then occupy and defend new lands to possess them legitimately.

While either narrative seems tenuous today, the United States and Canada inherited them, and they remain the legal basis for the claim to, and limit of, Native lands and peoples within the national borders of both countries. Both nations sought treaties with indigenous nations to gain their own sovereignty, but today Native nations use these same treaties to expand their sovereignty as autonomous governments on this very same basis. A good deal of colonial law serves to deny these Native American governments. Over time Canada established the Indian Act to define indigenous people as descended of an indigenous male; the United States, in decision, legislation, and policy, sought to destroy indigenous culture and communal land ownership. The shared effect was the depopulation of Native America.

When English settlers founded the Massachusetts Bay Colony in 1628, they discovered not the Virgin Land that their own stories prophesized, but what some scholars call a widowed land. In 1616 and 1618 plagues killed an estimated 90 percent of New England peoples. This human loss together with the depletion of game and fish may have left Massachusetts a relative wasteland. Down the coast Native American slaves helped restore labor populations: Native people of Carolina comprised about one-fourth of the slave population. Another epidemic in 1633 took the lives of key sachems and shook the balance of fur and wampum trade power in the region. Several bloody conflicts ensued, probably most notorious among them the Pequot War, which culminated in 1637, when English colonists and their Narragansett and Mohegan allies surrounded and set fire to a Pequot town near Mystic, Connecticut, then sold the survivors into slavery. The English forbade the use of the Pequot name to render them extinct. Later, North Americans viewed the demise of indigenous people as the sad though inevitable side effect of American Progress. He was the Vanishing American or, later, Indian. These colonial narratives— the Doctrine of Discovery, the Right of Conquest, the Virgin Land, the Ignoble Savage, the Noble Savage, and above all the Vanishing Indian—remain with us still today, and Native Americans variously employ and denounce such myths with their own literatures.

Such was the narrative landscape on the advent of settler colonies in North America. For centuries indigenous nations held territories and the government and economy to control them. Native peoples actively managed the land and its resources in a world wholly adequate to their needs. While Europeans boasted of advances in weapons and some other technologies, Native Americans held their own sense of greatness in other matters, such as government, architecture, and art. Indigenous people were not men in their primitive state, savages in need of evolution to European civilization; rather, they had their own differing civilizations. Long-held beliefs about the sanctity of land and life no doubt inculcated a special wisdom among Native Americans, but, like any human society, greed and waste and deception and malice were not unknown among them. Native Americans were both noble and ignoble "savages." Despite the conclusions among nineteenth-century North Americans that Native people were sadly destined to fall before the westbound tide of white settlers, the Indian did not vanish. Today we write and speak of Native Americans in the present tense: complex though ordinary people who as often gather a leafy medicine as carry a briefcase to court.

Just the facts

We cannot understand the emergence and value of Native American literature without this history of indigenous nations, and of European conquest and colonization. The latter is often a troubling history, but one that can instill pride and admiration in Native resistance, diplomacy, and adaptation in the midst of invasion. It merits restating that Native Americans negotiated the presence of Europeans and their threat to indigenous livelihood often through literary response, whether through testimony or address, essay or novel.

Anyone who lived during the early invasion of North America would be shocked to hear that Native American literature thrives today. And it thrives because Native people, despite the obstacles, are resilient. A 2010 census shows 2.9 million Native Americans in the United States and, in 2011, 1.4 million in Canada, with these numbers growing at a surprising rate. In Canada there are 600 indigenous nations, bands, or governments. The United States recognizes more than 550 Native American nations on more than 310 reservations that comprise more than 55 million acres of land. While some Native communities are still the poorest in North America and call for the greatest concern for social and health problems, many communities are growing their economies and reinvesting in cultural and language revitalization. Despite the challenges the future looks bright for indigenous North America.

Chapter 2
Oral literatures

Long ago in this world there was no land but only water. Above
in the Sky World a leader's daughter lay gravely ill, but a healer
dreamed the means to save her: the people must fell the tree that
provided the nation's food, then lay the girl at the foot of the tree.
After they did so, however, a young man stormed forward. He said
that it was wrong to destroy their food source to save their leader's
daughter, and he kicked her into the hole left by the uprooted tree.
Down she fell, but she was caught by a curious bird just before
hitting the water. The bird grew tired of carrying her, but a great
turtle took its place. After much discussion, the animals decided
that Sky Woman must have land on which to live. Toad
volunteered to dive down and retrieve mud to mound on Turtle's
back. Thus humans arrived on the land we now call Turtle Island.

Though variations on this "earth diver myth" have circulated
across North America for centuries, they did so orally. Native
Americans carefully trained their memories to record and
transmit vast bodies of knowledge verbatim because, in an oral
society, the known universe always stood only one generation from
loss. Indigenous tales instruct in ethics, ecology, religion, or
governance; still others record ancient migrations, catastrophes,
battles, and heroism. Oral literatures often form the basis of
Native American writing to this day, and so they begin the story
of Native literature in North America.

For centuries Iroquois people have experienced this story differently from the way we do as we read it from the printed page: they have long learned from Sky Woman's experience in their lodge of worship, the Longhouse, orally in an indigenous language, and among generations of related people using songs, rattles, and drums to enrich the tale's reception. Listeners to Sky Woman's story do not expect originality, but often they do offer varying interpretations of the story's meaning and ordering of the world.

Oral literatures grow from differing landscapes and their forms of life. Native Americans of the Pacific Northwest describe heroes such as Salmon Boy, who springs from a caught fish; on the Great Plains White Buffalo Calf Woman, and in the Southeast Corn Woman stand for sustenance itself and thus promises life. Despite their differences, oral literatures usually communicate a wish to live intimately with a unique ancestral land and its creatures, a commitment to a proper relationship with that land and its broad community, and a belief in the power of story to achieve this accordance. In a process that scholars term "world renewal," storytellers reaffirm their audiences' very understanding of their known universe.

Sky Woman helps build such a world. Humans accidentally enter another realm, where they would only drown without the help of the animals. Listeners learn they originate in the sky and must adapt to the demands of this other world. They share the leader's excruciating ethical dilemma: whether to lose his daughter or starve his people. He elects the former, only to have his authority rightly challenged by a younger leader. The story of Sky Woman thus conveys lessons in hierarchy, democratic community, and adaption of landscapes. That the animal people save and nurture Sky Woman invites trust in the earth's providence and affirms responsibilities to nonhuman populations. The first human is a solitary woman, thus declaring the centrality of women to Iroquois and other woodland peoples, who traditionally trace their descent and locate their homes through women. Such ancient relationships among communities, genders, and animals must be honored with trust and care through reciprocity. In telling and retelling the story of Sky Woman, Iroquois people hallow their relationship to this world while maintaining kinship with the spirit realm in the sky.

One day long ago a boy and his seven sisters were playing near the foot of a mountain. Suddenly the boy began grunting and scratching, and before their eyes he transformed into a bear. Terrified, the sisters climbed up the mountain, and the bear clawed after them, scoring the mountain with his fierce claws. Up and up the girls ascended until they reached the sky, where they remained as the stars of the Pleiades. The boy bear departed but the strange mountain known as Bear Lodge remains, tying the Kiowas to their migratory landscape through story. To this day they tell this tale to remember that they will always have relatives in the night sky. The storyteller seeks to depict this archetypal landscape, where the land and its inhabitants exist in complete order. Thus is Native American oral literature built not on fiction but indeed on truth, though of a special kind. In many indigenous philosophies, truth cannot be factually proven. Unlike many of us, Kiowas do not ask whether a boy really became a bear; rather, they confer truth by the understanding of the world that the story enables and protects. Often within this task the speaker can nonetheless improvise: some performers contend that Sky Woman was never kicked but fell, or even jumped. In this way, oral literature guards against dogma and sustains itself through adaptation.

Other indigenous creation narratives serve to categorize the world, its parts and interconnected taxonomies, through observation and testing. A Cherokee narrative posits a world beneath our own that one may reach through springs. They know this world experiences seasons opposite to ours because, whereas in summer a spring's water feels cool, in winter it flows warm.

Still other oral narratives advance a carefully prescribed ethics. For Blackfeet, Feather Woman married Sun and went to live with him in the sky. She missed her home terribly and one day, against Sun's threats, pulled the sacred turnip and climbed through the hole in the sky. Though sharing traits with Sky Woman's story, Feather Woman's narrative warns the people to be content with either this world or the spirit world, to honor the space between life and death. A long time ago some Sioux hunters saw a white buffalo calf transform into a beautiful young woman and approach them. When one lustful hunter tried to seize her, White Buffalo Calf Woman turned this man into a skeleton before the others' eyes, then communicated to his more respectful compatriots the sacred pipe ceremony. While this central story to the Sioux no doubt explains the origin of the pipe, it also teaches respect for women.

Oral philosophy

Nineteenth-century ethnographers often interpreted oral literatures through the era's Social Darwinist assumptions, as evidence that Native Americans existed "static" in a previous, "primitive" stage of human development up from which they could not "evolve." We now know that nothing could be further from the truth, that the oral tradition's ever-changing body of communally derived philosophy, in fact, challenges the very notion of stasis. Old ways and values have always required collective reflection and revision to thrive in an always changing world, and in today's world speakers transmit old tales both orally and in writing, and increasingly through graphic novels, film, and digital media; stories remain simultaneously new and authentic, and they continue to mix the real with the fantastic. Native people thus consciously shape their bodies of knowledge with new practices, values, and even languages, specifically to build ancient indigenous worldviews. For this reason we may best understand the growth of Native American oral literature as a process wherein performers consciously incorporate new conventions—even contradictory versions of a particular piece—within a flexible body of thought. Here knowledge is not the final identification of an unmediated truth, but an ongoing process in which storytellers and listeners may offer multiple perspectives. In this manner oral literature draws Native Americans into a culturally regulated center of knowledge.

The world-building power of oral literature relies on a particular conception of the imagination. Among many Native American peoples to imagine is not to see an illusion, but to manifest that which once did not exist. It is this understanding of the imagination that differs from narrower notions of the term. Popular usage often equates imagination with childish fantasy, or even with delusion. In its scientific and artistic use, however, imagination invites our capacity to see beyond our apparently limited world to solve problems or create art. Community members employing this version of the imagination to interpret their shared place in the land do not unconsciously rehearse a concretized script. To the contrary, they willfully reinvent their very world and their view of how best to belong to it.

Some writers describe this process as one that aligns two landscapes, one external and another internal. To many Native Americans, the external landscape includes not only the many elements of a certain region, such as the shape of a mountain or a bend in a river, the colors of rocks and soils, and its specific varieties of plants and animals, but also the subtle relationship among all elements. That totality might include the way a spring wind after a cool rain causes dogwood flowers to tremble, or the sound of shale sliding down a red clay canyon as bighorn sheep descend to greener grass in late winter. Native people tend to hold this external landscape and its close relationships as an inviolable order where the universe is always whole, pure, and complete.

The interior landscape is that place where perceptions, ideas, and beliefs reside. Because Native Americans are often profoundly influenced by their ancestral homelands, this internal landscape bears the above relationships and, in fact, forms a mirror-like reflection of that exterior landscape. Even among Native people, however, such template-like overlays of mind and land are viewed as ideal: that perfect state of being in which one exists in balance with these two realms, a state often described as harmony or beauty. In pursuit of this harmony, a singer or storyteller invites communal participation in a people's oral literature, where, if successful, listeners discover a profound sense of well-being and delight. This state of bliss between mind and land creates mental, even physical, wellness. Many Native Americans also view narratives to exist in three epochs: a primordial time when the world was young, godlike spirits moved about, humans still were not fully formed, and animals were humanlike and could even speak; a transitional time, when the land settled into its present existence and life forms became more assigned to their present condition; and historical time, when Native Americans can recall through historical memory events such as migrations, wars, and great leaders, and, of course, vernacular or humorous tales.

To align these interior and exterior landscapes, Native Americans often enlist ritual dramas. These include narrative and song but can also include oratory, through which a nation may attempt to control natural and supernatural forces, as in the request for rain, for instance. Such dramatic performances, delivered in special archaic language and style, can be fabulously creative, as in the Pacific Northwest, where performers don costumes that transform them into deities as they enact the story of origin. Navajos maintain a large body of ritual dramas, often to heal the ill. In the Night Chant a healer leads a ritual that begins at sunset and ends eight and a half days later. For the first four days, songs help to purify the afflicted. At midnight on the fourth day deities descend and touch the sick person, to impart their power. On the ninth day the healer calls the thunder; the songs from the previous eight days are repeated throughout the final night. At sunrise on the tenth day the afflicted person faces east and is healed. Consider this portion of a prayer from the ceremony's third night of purification: "Happily may I walk. / Happily with abundant dark clouds may I walk. / Happily with abundant showers may I walk. / Happily with abundant plants may I walk. / Happily on a trail of pollen may I walk." In the repetition of key features that suggest emotional restoration and natural replenishment, the singer requests a healthy, mobile body defined by graceful movement over a verdant land. In other ceremonies such as the Iroquois Condolence Ceremony, ritual drama restores the coherence of the confederacy on a leader's death. Society here becomes a grieving widow whose eyes are filled with tears and whose throat is clogged with ashes from a dead fire in a dark home. Such death and grief threaten insanity, and so the oration washes the eyes of the grieving, in the metaphor that sustains this extensive ritual drama.

Because they form such a part of narratives and ritual dramas, indigenous songs comprise the largest part of oral literatures. Navajos pray by singing, and they strengthen their prayer-songs with melody, rhythm, and multiple voices. Other Native American peoples turn to song when words alone are not enough to complete a prayer. Among Salishes, drums or rattles usually accompany songs taught to a singer through contact with supernatural forces.

Among Papagos, one must perform an act of heroism then fast for a vision that may contain an empowering or supernatural song. Among Hopis and Shoshonis, songs belong to the group as a whole, but for Papagos, families and even individuals can own and transfer songs. Because songs serve to restore indigenous minds to the order of ancestral lands, they often invoke an enchanted landscape, as in this Yaqui deer song: "You are an enchanted flower wilderness world, / you are an enchanted wilderness world, / you lie with see-through freshness. / You are an enchanted wilderness world, / you lie with see-through freshness, / wilderness world." While some songs invoke the land's mystical power, others celebrate major events such as naming, puberty, death, and remembrance. This Tlingit song for mourning compares the departed to a drifting log: "I always compare you to a drifting log with iron nails in it. Let my / brother float in, in that way. Let him float ashore on a good sandy / beach." The haunting image imagines a shipwrecked brother lost at sea and finally moored in a way that brings peace to mourners.

A related genre can be found in Native American speech or oratory. Europeans have long admired indigenous speaking abilities, and training to speak publicly was a part of the early education of many Native peoples. Recognizing this artistry at surrenders and treaty gatherings, Europeans began to translate such speeches, which were often elegies. Such translations, however, differed at times from the original statements. For this reason experts often view translations of elegies nostalgic about indigenous defeat and disappearance with an appreciative though discriminating eye. Through oral enactments found in story, ritual drama, song, and elegy, Native Americans renew relationships with each other, with other creatures, and with the land. Though we should not assume a seamless continuum between oral performance and contemporary Native literature, we might place oral literatures at the heart of plans for world renewal, from colonization to the present.

Heroes and monsters

The trouble started with a jealous Sun. When she daily passed under the rim of the bowl in the sky, the people never greeted her but made ugly faces when they squinted. She complained to her brother Moon, who replied that the people smiled up at him every night. Angrily she shone down on the people, and the people suffered and died under her heat. Desperately they called on friendly deities, the Little Men. The Little Men plotted to kill Sun when she visited with her daughter at midday. They turned three humans into snakes and sent them up to wait at the door of Sun's daughter's house. The door opened and Copperhead struck— killing the daughter by accident. Sun hid in the house and grieved, and now the people suffered not from heat but from utter darkness. The Little Men advised that the only way to bring out Sun was to bring back her daughter from the Darkening Land to the west.

The people selected seven men, and the Little Men told each to carry a sourwood rod. They were instructed that, when they found Sun's daughter dancing they must strike her until she fell from the circle. They should push her into a box and carry her to her mother, Sun. They must never open the box even a crack. For seven days the men walked until arriving at the Darkening Land, where they did find the dead dancing. When Sun's daughter danced by they struck her seven times before she fell, then quickly dropped her in the box and fled unnoticed. On their trek east she wept from within the box. The girl cried for food and then she begged for air; she said she would soon die. Would not they open the box just a crack? The men relented and opened a slit in the box, then heard a whoosh and saw a redbird stream by. They returned home to find the box empty, and for their failure humans cannot recover their friends from the Darkening Land. Sun continued to bow her head and cry, and her tears caused great floods until the people sent dancers up with songs to entertain her. At last when a drummer changed the song, Sun looked up, saw the beautiful dancers, and finally smiled.

Perhaps second in importance to the origin story within oral literatures is that of the culture hero. In this Cherokee story, in some primordial time the people suffer a misunderstanding with their deity Sun. For their foolishness they are made further to anguish. Only a special person, often divinely chosen, is capable of questing to other mysterious worlds, accomplishing feats or battling monsters, and returning with the resource to save the people—often it is fire or water. Here, the Little Men, though divine, try and fail, indeed worsen the situation with Sun. The bungled plan can be repaired only by human heroes. They dare travel well beyond their known world and, in the longer epic, encounter strange people and stranger customs, dance with and trick the dead, and transgress Sun in capturing her daughter. Like

27

many heroes the world over, these Cherokee heroes bear a tragic flaw. They defy the Little Men's instructions and open the box, freeing the girl and thus failing to appease Sun. But this narrative also holds a lesson. Readers no doubt share the torment of the men when they must hear the haunting cry from a child trapped in a box. The men's compassion bursts forth and they free her, allowing listeners to ponder when we should or should not compromise our humanity for the sake of a mission. Last, only dance and song end Sun's grief, reminding Cherokees that world renewal—like story itself—ensures lasting resources like Sun. Today Cherokees still dance about the fire, the embodiment of Sun, to help her raise her head and smile.

In their ability to travel to unknown lands, heroes celebrate a fundamental quality among many Native peoples that, on first thought, may seem to contradict the creation narrative itself. If origin narratives confirm ancestral place, would not travel risk its undermining? Hero narratives, however, may be understood to complement oral emergences from ancestral lands by inviting indigenous minds to think beyond familiar environments and investigate other worlds where one learns from strange places, then returns home to offer that new knowledge to the people.

Long ago when the world was still dark, Giant disguised himself in a raven skin and left the Sky World. His father gave him a stone that he dropped into the sea, where it rose into a rock on which he landed. He flew to the mainland and scattered salmon roe and trout roe and a sea-lion bladder full of fruits to enrich the earth. But the world was still dark except for a few stars in the night, and the people could barely see to gather the food. So Giant decided to return to the Sky World to steal the light. He put on his raven skin and ascended, squeaking through a hole into the sky, then removed his disguise and waited by a spring near the house of the Sky World's leader. Soon the leader's daughter came to fetch water. Giant transformed himself into a cedar leaf and floated on the water, and the daughter scooped him up and drank. By and by she

28

was pregnant and bore a child who cried day and night to play with the box in which the leader kept the daylight. After a few days of play, the baby (who was Giant of course) snatched up the light and fled for the hole, donned his raven skin, and flew to the mainland, where far below some men were fishing. Giant asked for a fish but they called him a liar, recognizing him as Giant merely disguised as a raven. Giant then threatened to break open the box. They refused, he broke it open, and light burst forth throughout the land.

Tsimshians retell this hero narrative of Raven to recall not only how the world was made but also the heroism that enabled it. Here the treasured resource of light itself, as in the Cherokees story, involves a theft. And like many other heroes of Native American oral literature, he moves from the Sky World to the earth world, from bird to human, and man to child, through a symbolic rebirth. In many such stories cunning, deception, and theft win the day, to confirm persistence of folly and subversion within even the most divine events.

In other such narratives heroes possess rare talents. A couple once had a child who seemed old beyond her years, and who sat day after day creating the most beautiful garments made of porcupine quills. On their completion she packed them up and, despite her parents' refusals, walked to the horizon. Days later she came upon a strange lodge, entered, and unpacked the seven sets of clothes before a boy with a mysterious medicine. Soon his six brothers returned home to find their handsome clothes. Perhaps jealous the buffalo people again and again attacked the lodge to demand the boys return their new sister, but they refused. When they would surely be destroyed, the brothers called on their youngest to use his medicine. All climbed a tree, and the buffalo rammed it, nearly knocking it down. The boy shot a magic arrow into the tree and it began to grow. He shot another arrow and again it grew. On the fourth arrow the tree had reached the clouds, where all jumped free. The little brother then turned all into the stars of the Big Dipper. In hero narratives such as this Cheyenne story, the child hero is preternaturally talented, even to the point of defying her parents or leaders. So doing, these heroes model a pattern of individual dissent from the greater community, but which ultimately heals, saves, or imparts new knowledge to that community.

But what would such heroes do without their monsters? Long ago the land became overrun by war, and people starved and grew miserable. Many lost their humanity and turned cannibal, preying on their former friends. Peacemaker set out to end the violence and bring the people together under one longhouse. On his travels he came upon a lonely cabin, climbed the roof, and looked down the smoke hole to see a snake-haired man stirring a pot filled with human flesh. Peacemaker gazed into the pot and saw the

3. This contemporary depiction of the Hiawatha wampum belt, *Words and Memory, Pollination Understands Movements*, by Eric Gansworth S·ha-weñ na-sae², retells the story of Peacemaker's creation of the Iroquois Confederacy. Each square represents a nation, with the tree of peace and fire at the center.

reflection of his own face. The cannibal then peered into his steaming swill and saw Peacemaker. It was not his own hateful scowl, but a clear-eyed and handsome face. In that moment the cannibal read in those pure features who he had been and could be again: a fully human being who reasoned beyond self-interest for the good of all. Peacemaker climbed down from the roof, entered the house, and soon brought the cannibal to what Iroquois people call the "good mind." To Iroquois people such a story confirms the view that monsters display the ugly side of human nature, but that even the most hateful can be returned to community.

Trickster teachings

In what are often called trickster tales, indigenous oral literatures employ a crafty character who threatens moral tenets, defeats enemies with cunning and deception, besmirches the sacred, and even refuses to die. In the Southeast he is Rabbit, near the Great Lakes he is Nanabozho, on the Great Plains he is Spider, on the northern plains Old Man, in Canada he is Wolverine and Jay, in the Pacific Northwest he is Raven, and in the Southwest and plateau region he is Coyote. Wherever she or he operates (among Hopis she is usually female), Trickster entertains with uproariously bad behavior that listeners consume for pleasure. Still today at the bare mention of Coyote Native Americans might burst into laughter. But why is Trickster such a part of indigenous creation narratives? With folly and blunder, profanity and immorality, he expresses that other human urge toward chaos that is also potentially wildly productive. In this way Trickster brings balance to the Native cosmos.

They say that long ago a terrible winter was causing a famine in the settlement. One by one the people starved and died, and their relatives summoned the last of their strength to hoist their bodies onto scaffolds for burial, as was the custom. Coyote came loping through the deep snow, starving like the people. He stopped at the cemetery and began to sniff around the scaffold, when a dead person spoke to him, inviting him to leap up on the scaffold and visit. The rotting body asked how the body smelled. Coyote replied that he smelled like a delicious rabbit stew. Coyote licked the body. The dead man asked him again how he smelled, and Coyote said that he smelled like a savory chunk of deer meat. Coyote nibbled on the body. Again the dead man asked, and Coyote mumbled that he smelled like a delectable pile of buffalo ribs, and Coyote tore into the putrid flesh. In this manner Coyote ate until the snow melted and the trees flowered. In his shiny, fat coat Coyote lay in the sun beside the pile of chewed bones, when again the dead man asked how he smelled. Coyote jumped up and snarled that he smelled like nothing but a worthless, stinking corpse! Enraged, the skeleton suddenly stood and chased Coyote into the sunset.

This Winnebago story uses dark humor to invite listeners to meditate on a serious moral issue. Today's readers might struggle to imagine famine but, as this story is very old, it no doubt hearkens to a time when it was often on the minds of those suffering a long winter with dwindling food stores. Coyote thus warns community members about the temptation for ethical transgressions in desperate times. In the story Coyote in his gluttonous, selfish imagination, wishes to believe that the corpse is legitimate food, and even befriends it. When winter subsides and food is plentiful, however, Coyote betrays his friendship. In this manner the Trickster narrative, through humor and even horror, invites listeners to consider the darkness in their own humanity.

Yet while Trickster displays the worst of human behavior, he as often shows Native Americans how to be courageous and cunning to solve daily problems or even to resist attacks on their very lives. Coyote was walking one day when he ran into Old Woman, who said that he should be careful: there was a giant nearby. Coyote boasted that giants did not scare him, though, in fact, he had never met one. While whistling a tune he found a fallen branch and scooped it up for a club with which to kill the giant. Soon he entered a cave and stumbled upon a starving woman who pleaded for food. She told Coyote that he had entered not a cave but the giant's mouth. Soon he found other people trapped in the giant's mouth, and the woman told him that there was no escape, as the giant's belly was as big as the entire valley. Unfazed he travelled to the giant's belly, then took out his knife and cut meat from its walls to feed the trapped people, who had never thought of that. Now fed, the people asked Coyote how they should escape the giant. Coyote concluded that he would stab the giant in the heart. Looking about he saw a distant volcano, and surmised that it was the giant's heart. Coyote stabbed and stabbed the giant's heart, warning the people that when the giant began to die there would be an earthquake and the giant would open his mouth. The volcano began to erupt and the lava, the giant's blood, began to spew forth. The giant opened his mouth and the people escaped, thanks to Coyote.

In this final Trickster story told among Salishes, Coyote is a strategist who sees beyond immediate perceptions to solve greater problems: the starving people do not think to look about them to gain a more encompassing picture of their troubled land where giants or invaders rule. With his gift of insight and his sneaky and plotting nature Coyote saves the world.

4. On the seal of the Massachusetts Bay Company, an Indian pleads: "Come over and help us."

Chapter 3
To write in English

"Come over and help us!" the Indian pleads. The 1628 seal of the Massachusetts Bay Company depicts this Indian with a speech bubble, an allusion to Acts 16:9, in which Paul dreams that heathens invite his Gospel into their lands. The English colonies answered this apocryphal invitation with what they called civilization, including literacy and Christianity for indigenous people. Because missionaries sought to bring their Bible to Native Americans, the first publications in North America relied on the literary translations of Native people. Indeed missionary John Eliot never could have produced his "Indian library," the first major North American publishing house, without the help of translators such as Montaukett Cockenoe-de-Long Island, Job Nesuton, who was Massachusett, and Nipmuck James Printer.

Missionaries soon taught their "Praying Indians" to write in their Algonquian languages to distribute the Gospel, but by the middle seventeenth century literate Native Americans began to write for their own communities as well. Cockenoe-de-Long Island drafted deeds for Massachusetts land settlements, and James Printer served as King Philip's official scribe and probably recorded the release of white captive Mary Rowlandson in 1676. By the 1660s Native people attended Harvard, and by the American Revolution hundreds of Native American students had attended the College

of William and Mary, Dartmouth College, and what became
Princeton University.

In the wake of the religious revival known as the Great Awakening in
the 1740s leaders such as John Sargeant Sr. and Eleazar Wheelock
intensified Eliot's earlier plan for the Praying Indian villages, where
Native children remained with their families to worship and learn.
These religious leaders discovered that Native American students
learned better when far from the influence of their families. They
thus designed the first manual labor Indian residential and boarding
schools. The schools, such as Moor's Indian Charity School, started
by Wheelock, sought to expunge indigenous culture through
religious conversion, hard work, and literacy in English. This model
of Native American education remained into the twentieth century.

Such schools produced the first Native American writers and the
first advocates for Native rights. Mohegans Samson Occom and
Joseph Johnson, who studied at Moor's, and Mahican Hendrick
Aupaumut, who attended Sargeant's school, became fully capable in
western ways and English literacy. These Native American leaders
produced some of the first autobiographies and sermons in English.

On a stormy September day in 1772 in New Haven before a crowd
of Europeans, Africans, and Natives, Occom, now an ordained
minister, delivered "A Sermon, Preached at the Execution of
Moses Paul, an Indian." Occom describes what we today recognize
as a plague of alcoholism among colonized peoples.
"Drunkenness," he explains, "has brought this destruction and
untimely death upon him." Alcoholism strips "us of every desirable
comfort in this life; by this we are poor, miserable and wretched;
by this sin we have no name of credit in the world among polite
nations; for this sin we are despised in the world, and it is all right
and just, for we despise ourselves more; and if we don't regard
ourselves, who will regard us?" Occom exhorts Native people to
refuse the weapons of their destruction—the colonizer's liquor—to
recover their lives and revitalize their nations. His call begins a

tradition of Native American intellectualism seeking to empower members of the community, where colonial resistance must begin, for "if we don't regard ourselves, who will regard us?" Occom's sermon became a bestseller and is thought to be the first publication in English by a Native person.

These first Native American writers retained many of their indigenous views. Occom and Johnson eventually grew disillusioned with Wheelock, and in 1774 Johnson secured New York land from the Oneidas to establish their own Praying Indian village, entirely indigenous in inhabitance and governance. In his speech to the Oneidas Johnson too invokes alcohol as an emblem of colonial trickery, and he beseeches audiences to sober up from the previous era's trust of the English: "Whilst our forefathers were blind, ignorant, yea drowned in Spirituous Liquors; the English stript them, yea they as it were cut off their Right hands; and now we their Children [are] just...coming to our Senses, like one that has been drunk." Johnson's Brothertown settlement became a refuge for Oneidas during the Revolutionary War and, under the leadership of Aupaumut, other Native Americans settled nearby at Stockbridge. Around 1790 Aupaumut wrote one of the earliest Native historical pieces in which he, like Occom and Johnson, uses his literacy in English to assert the autonomous, pre-Christian civilization of his Stockbridge people.

Native American protest

During the Second Great Awakening, in the 1820s, African Americans and Native people joined with Protestant clergy to attack such social ills as drunkenness, slavery, and the Indian Removal Act, which Congress passed in 1830 to force all Native Americans west of the Mississippi. In the 1830s emerged a Native voice so perceptive and trenchant it would not be rivaled until the 1960s. Pequot minister William Apess was born in 1798 in Colrain, Massachusetts, and, after his parents separated in 1801, he was given to his grandparents. In 1802 his intoxicated grandmother beat him so badly that the town selectmen apprenticed him to a white family nearby. Apess had memories as a child of abuse and abandonment, perhaps in concert with local prejudices, that left him afraid of the mere sight of a Native person. In his autobiography *A Son of the Forest* (1829) he describes happening upon darkly tanned European women, whom he mistakes for Native Americans, and flees in terror. There he also tells of becoming lost in the woods, where he shrinks in fear of the imagined savage non-Christian inhabitants.

After living with several white families and repeatedly running away, Apess enlisted in the War of 1812 as a drummer boy. In 1815 he mustered out of the army and traveled through Canada, eventually making his way home to Connecticut on foot. Apess was reunited with his aunt, Sally George, who practiced both

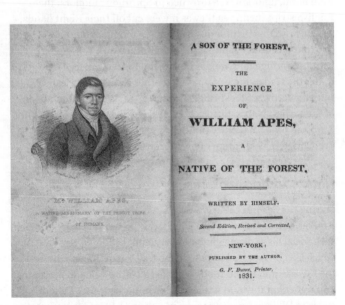

5. A portrait of the urbane William Apess, printed as the frontispiece of his self-published *A Son of the Forest* (second edition, 1831). Until 1837 he spelled his name "Apes."

Pequot lifeways and Christianity, and he was baptized during a Methodist meeting in 1818. He started a family and became an itinerant missionary and, after his application for a preacher's license was declined by the Methodist Episcopal Church, was ordained by the dissenting Protestant Methodist Church in 1831. When Apess visited the Mashpee community of Cape Cod, he became an ardent supporter of their "Woodland Revolt" against Massachusetts to retain their ancestral land. With his impassioned protest writing in his *Indian Nullification of the Unconstitutional Laws of Massachusetts Relative to the Marshpee Tribe* (1835), Apess helped Mashpees become one of the few Native American groups to preserve their autonomy during the disastrous removal era.

In a slim book, *The Experiences of Five Christian Indians of the Pequot Tribe* (1833), Apess celebrates the conversion of Pequot women. This book's appended essay, "An Indian's Looking-Glass for the White Man," fulminates against European Christian hypocrisy:

> Assemble all nations together in your imagination, and then let the whites be seated among them.... Now suppose these skins were put together, and each skin had its national crimes written upon it— which skin do you think would have the greatest?... I know that when I cast my eye upon that white skin, and if I saw those crimes written upon it, I should enter my protest against it immediately and cleave to that which is more honorable.

Apess directly addresses white people by name, demanding they look upon themselves to confront the Christian hypocrisy of believing in a God that favors Europeans over all others. Yet he also harnesses Christianity's promise of human equality to "seat" whites with other peoples at a desegregated table, then images the power of writing to expose the denied crimes of colonialism and slavery that rely on the failed logic of race. Apess's spectacle of crime-written flesh shocks readers to this day. Here the marks of savagery do not appear as indigenous tattoos or slave brands on African bodies; rather, through literacy, Apess claims Native American rights and envisions colonial crimes writ bodily as well. Nothing quite like it reappears for more than a century.

Apess wrote two other books: one, a sermon on the misguided though then-popular theory that indigenous people are descended from a lost tribe of Israel, and another on King Philip's War. In 1675 Metacom, or King Philip, led the Wampanoag Confederacy against the Puritans. In *Eulogy on King Philip* (1836), Apess incorrectly imagines his descent from Metacom to remind North Americans that all are equal in the eyes of God. In his autobiography he plainly states, "the blood of a king is no better than that of the subject. We are in fact but one family; we are all the descendants of one great progenitor—Adam." Apess lionizes Metacom, a supposed villain in the American story, to reclaim a history—and thus a humanity—for indigenous peoples thought to be caught in a savage state and without a record of their national past. So doing Apess remains the standard-bearer of protest writing that reclaims indigenous history for indigenous rights.

This genre of alternative Native American history became invaluable during the removal era, when North American proponents classified Native people as incapable of being educated. Because Native Americans did not *individually* own or cultivate the earth, the argument went, whites had a "preemptive right" to their lands. In 1826 the federal government supported the disputed Treaty of Buffalo Creek by which the Ogden Land Company gained huge tracts of land in central New York. Senecas and their Quaker allies protested, and the Seneca orator Red Jacket went to Washington to repudiate the fraudulent document. The Senate refused to intervene and the Ogden Land Company began selling Seneca lands to whites.

About this time Tuscarora intellectual David Cusick published his indigenous national history, *Sketches of Ancient History of the Six*

Nations. Cusick displayed an unusual intellect even as a child: in 1803 a missionary describes visiting the Buffalo Creek Reservation, where the boy was cherished as a prodigy in drawing and painting. Cusick was reluctant to convey Iroquois notions of history, which were "involved with fables" that cannot be divorced from historical fact, as western readers might have demanded. He nonetheless pressed on to write the first history in English by a Native person, wherein the story of the universe includes the "holder of the heavens" and "stonish giants" who brutalize the first settlers of the Six Nations, or Iroquois homeland. Like Apess, Cusisk is aware of white perceptions about Native Americans as superstitious savages. Cusick argues the merit of Iroquois oral history on the basis that, not unlike biblical parable, it serves to build a universe, resolve peoplehood, explain relationships with land and other life forms, and establish the sovereign status of indigenous nations. With this ultimate purpose Cusick uses oral history to affirm the sacred origin of the Iroquois's government, and thus their spiritual but especially legal rights to their homeland.

Other Iroquois intellectuals shared in the peaceful though vociferous resistance to the Buffalo Creek Treaty. Occom's lecture tours in England generated funds for later Seneca writer Maris Bryant Pierce to attend Moor's Indian Charity School, which later became Dartmouth College. Pierce recognized the flawed nature of arguments for Indian removal, the primary one being that Native Americans cannot be westernized. His writings reverse colonial relations to gain a moment of political leverage and moral authority. In his *Address on the Present Condition and Prospects of the Aboriginal Inhabitants of North America* (1838), delivered in a Baptist church in Buffalo in August 1838, Pierce asks:

> Say, if some beings from fairy land, or some distant planet, should
> come to you in such a manner as to cause you to deem them children
> of *greater light* and *superior wisdom* to yourselves, and you should
> open to them the hospitality of your dwellings and the *fruits* of your
> *labor*, and they should, by dint of their *superior wisdom* dazzle and

41

amaze you, so as for what to them were *toys and rattles* they should gain freer admission and fuller welcome, till finally they should claim the *right* to your possessions and of hunting you, like wild beasts, from your long and hitherto undisputed domain, how ready would *you* be to be taught of *them.*—How cordially would you open your *minds* to the conviction that they meant not to deceive you *further* and still more fatally in their proffers of pretended kindness.

Here Pierce not only invites self-reflection among North American settlers but also gives reason for the reluctance among Native Americans to assume the "manners and customs" of their conquerors. Other Seneca intellectuals argued in support of their emigration west, beyond the interference of white settlers. Nathaniel Thayer Strong was a European-educated and converted "Young Chief" like Pierce, served as the interpreter for the Buffalo Creek Treaty signing, and supported removal. In his *Appeal to the Christian Community on the Condition and Prospects of the New York Indians* (1841), Strong describes Native peoples as "feeble remnants of once powerful nations" who face "impending extinction." Like other pro-removal Native Americans, Thayer views emigration as the only choice for the survival of indigenous nations.

Talking leaves

When missionary Samuel Worcester arrived at the Brainerd Mission in Chattanooga, Tennessee, in 1825 to make Cherokees "English in their language, civilized in their habits, and Christian in their religion," he was dismayed to discover that they were already literate—in their own language.

Around 1815 a middle-aged Cherokee silversmith began work on a project that soon consumed his every waking hour. Sequoyah had sat with friends who marveled that Europeans communicated without speech across distances with their "talking leaves." Some wondered whether the Creator had given them this gift or if they themselves invented it. Sequoyah believed the latter and, picking up some charcoal and a piece of wood, began making a sign for horse. The men laughed but the conversation sparked his mind and he soon set to work. Sequoyah had an impaired leg that increasingly bound him to his cabin in Wills Valley, Alabama, where he became more dedicated to his many drawings. He had a white father whom he had never met, he spoke no English, and he could neither read nor write. Possessing no models for the understanding of writing, he nonetheless imagined a system by which a symbol could indicate a sound. Having no pen, ink, or paper, he carved marks into wood with a knife. Later he carved a pen, learned that it needed a groove to hold the ink, and concocted his own ink from Poke berries.

Though Sequoyah faced severe censure by his local community, he eventually isolated 86 sounds by characters to complete his syllabary. He tested his system with his daughter, Ahyokah, and she quickly mastered it, but when he attempted to introduce the syllabary to his countrymen, they scoffed and ridiculed him as a fool or, worse, a witch, so he devised a new plan. In 1821 he traveled to the Cherokee settlements in Arkansas, showed them his daughter's skill, and won their approval to train some students there. In a short time Sequoyah had taught these students to write, and so convinced a local leader in Arkansas to dictate to him a letter to a close friend in the Cherokee Nation in the east.

They sealed the letter with wax and Sequoyah carried the letter with him back to Willstown in Alabama to deliver it in person, where he assembled some of the Nation's most recognized men, broke the letter's seal, and read the message from distant Arkansas. Sequoyah had single-handedly invented a written language, an extremely rare accomplishment anywhere in the world. For his invention he won the status of "beloved man" of the Cherokee Nation. Citizens embraced his gift and orders for pen, ink, and paper flooded the Indian agent; soon Sequoyan could be found written in charcoal on buildings, carved into trees, and used in the notes passed among Cherokee students in mission schools.

Writing removal

In 1828 Elias Boudinot penned the first issue of North America's first newspaper in an indigenous language, the *Cherokee Phoenix*. The paper declared in English and Cherokee the vital role that American literacy will play in transforming Native people: "[We hope] for that happy period, when all the Indian tribes of America shall arise, Phoenix like, from their ashes, and when the terms, 'Indian depredation,' 'war-whoop,' 'scalping knife' and the like, shall become obsolete, and forever be 'buried deep underground.'" Though Boudinot wished to make some symbols of supposed savagery "obsolete," he does so by retaining other time-honored Native American symbols, such as the Cherokee's central fire of worship, and that of international peace between "Indian tribes of America" and North Americans, the Indian hatchet "buried deep underground."

By the early nineteenth century Enlightenment's "civilization policy" had crumbled beneath a romantic version of nationalism and the invention of racial difference. Indians were now viewed as uneducable and doomed to extinction; their only hope, argued supporters of Indian removal, was preservation in the West beyond the reach of civilization. Indigenous nations hatched a different plan. They sought to adapt those European values that encouraged their overpowering invaders to see them as sufficiently civilized to own their ancestral lands. At the same time they attempted to convey their legal and cultural autonomy as self-governing nations. In 1824 Cherokees informed President John Quincy Adams: "The arts of civilized life have been successfully introduced among us; we consider ourselves permanently settled and no inducement can ever prompt us to abandon our habitations for a distant, wild, and strange clime."

Though the U.S. government recognized Cherokee sovereignty, it also promised the state of Georgia that it would extinguish all Indian claims to land within Georgia's claimed borders. On the discovery of gold around 1830, Georgians flooded into Cherokee lands, and Georgia passed laws to eclipse the Cherokee government. Cherokees could not legislate and could not testify in Georgia courts, and non-Cherokees could not reside in the Cherokee Nation. The Georgia Guard removed missionaries "chained with horses' trace-chains around their necks and fastened, one to the neck of a horse, the other to the tail of the cart." Cherokees pleaded with the federal government to uphold their treaty promising to defend Cherokees against states' intrusions, but Andrew Jackson replied, "You can live on your lands in Georgia if you choose, but I cannot interfere with the laws of that state to protect you."

Cherokee leaders carried their cause to the Supreme Court. In 1831, in *Cherokee Nation v. Georgia*, Chief Justice John Marshall determined that, because the United States had made treaties with Indian tribes, the United States had implicitly recognized the tribes' capacity to govern, and thus their nationhood. But because Indian tribes were within the borders of the United States they were not foreign. And because the tribes had accepted the protection of the federal government, they were in a state of "pupilage" to the United States. Indian tribes were thus "domestic dependent" nations, as Marshall coined the ambiguous phrase. Other officials worked further to diminish the nation status of Indian tribes. Promoting removal, Secretary of War Lewis Cass published a report on the southeastern Indians insisting that "government is unknown among them....They are in a state of nature, as much so as it is possible for any people to be."

Aware of the threats underlying such fictions, Native American intellectuals became good negotiators of complex ideas regarding representation, nation, race, and culture. One strategy was to seek education from western institutions to be recognized as rational agents with a government and a nation. By the late 1820s, almost all Cherokees could write in Sequoyan and, with the eventual success of missionary schools, many could speak, read, and write English. Citizens such as Elias Boudinot departed for Cornwall Mission School in Connecticut and returned to establish the national newspaper. His cousin John Ridge also left for Cornwall and came back a lawyer. Others, such as David Brown, returned from Andover in Maine to lead the Moral and Literary Society of the Cherokee Nation. The Cherokee Nation appointed such intellectuals as delegates to Washington, where they gained support from the likes of Henry Clay, Daniel Webster, and William Wirt. These and other Cherokee diplomats operated comfortably within their own and foreign cultures, and, in fact, they consciously reshaped their national identity precisely through such interaction. Such Cherokee cosmopolitans viewed their adaptation of European ways as fundamental to their ever-changing nationhood, not as their corruption by civilization, and through their increasingly international literatures they protected that nationhood.

In an 1828 lecture at the First Presbyterian Church in Philadelphia Boudinot declares the distinct ancestral place of the Cherokee Nation, on the one hand, and, with its sublime vistas, its ability to nurture their "Americanness," on the other. Employing what one scholar calls the Cherokee "discourse of rural virtue," Boudinot rapturously exhorts: "Those lofty and barren mountains give to us that free air and pure water which distinguish our country." And later: "The government, though defective in many respects, is well suited to the condition of the inhabitants. As they rise in information and refinement, changes in it must follow, until they arrive at that state of advancement, when I trust they will be admitted into all the privileges of the American family."

Boudinot asks not for U.S. citizenship but for international exchange. In Jacksonian America the ambiguity between the national and the foreign was only exacerbated by *Cherokee Nation v. Georgia*, which classified Indians as neither foreign nationals nor U.S. citizens. Cherokee writers thus used their originary view of kinship and their new status as "domestic" nations to open up and enter that American family. Swiftly employing this rhetoric in address and journalism, they humanized Cherokee communities as similar to U.S. society and, because they were similar, worthy of sympathy and protection.

Cherokee writers were encouraged by their government not only to represent the cultural, religious, and industrial so-called improvements in the Cherokee Nation, but also to educate the North American public about tribal customs. While some leaders, such as Principal Chief John Ross, wished openly to preserve Cherokee national lifeways, Cherokee citizens felt pressure from their mission-funding sources to portray indigenous habits as retrograde and dwindling, even if such practices were alive and well. For this reason the writings of missionaries and students often conflict. In 1828 a Cherokee mission student named Sally Reece writes to a benefactor in Boston:

> First I will tell you about the Cherokees. I think they improve. They have a printing press, and print a paper which is called the *Cherokee Phoenix*. They come to meeting on Sabbath days. They wear clothes which they made themselves. Some though rude, have shoes and stockings. They keep horses, cows, sheep, and swine. Some have oxen. They cultivate fields. They have yet a great many bad customs but I hope all these will soon be done away.

Reece already understands exactly how to negotiate colonial relations. She begins by acknowledging the progress narrative of the civilization program, then affirms the literacy of the nation, leaving those unaware of the Cherokee language to assume they are learning English. She speaks as though actions or dress alone, especially where they concern church attendance and shoes, determine progress. These, along with husbandry and cultivated fields of not corn but wheat, ensure that the Indians are coming to resemble an American family, Reece seems to promise.

Meanwhile, the missionaries grew restless. In their private writings they complain about Cherokees walking in single file, men leading the women, they said, in case of attack. Missionaries censored their own portrayals of ceremonial dances that "depend mostly upon a variety of obscene gestures and movements which will not bear description." By 1835 only about 10 percent of

Cherokees belonged to a church; all others worshipped traditionally. So Cherokees like Elias Boudinot practiced a kind of double consciousness. They characterize their extant tribalism carefully to reduce its threat to Christian society, ensuring its similarity to North American culture and its certain demise: "Most of our readers probably know what is meant by Indian clans. It is no more than a division of an Indian tribe into large families. But it was the mutual law of clans as connected with murder, which rendered this custom savage and barbarous. We speak of what it was once, not as it is now, for the Cherokee abolished it," as it read in the *Cherokee Phoenix*. They did, at least on paper, in 1810.

Cherokee writers naturalized Cherokee cultural tradition even as they showcased Cherokee evolution. Like Lewis Cass, who insisted that Indians' "habits were stationary and unbending; never changing with the changing circumstances," many North Americans understood Native people to be outside of time. They were representations of the past in the present. In popular views, Native Americans would inevitably "melt away" before the tide of America's progress, a civilization evolving *in time*. To overturn this misperception, as well as to advance their nationhood, Cherokees worked to place their people *in time*, consciously modifying their world and their lives, as did the North Americans.

Boudinot began his public lecture thus: "Some there are, who at the bare sight of an Indian, would throw back their imaginations to ancient times, to the ravages of savage warfare. What is an Indian? Is he not formed of the same materials with yourself? For 'of one blood God created all the nations that dwell on the face of the earth.' Though it be true that he is ignorant, that he is a heathen, that he is a savage; yet he is no more than all others have been under similar circumstances. Eighteen centuries ago what were the inhabitants of Great Britain? I now stand before you to assist in raising my native country to an equal standing with other nations of the earth." Here meeting the myth of racial difference head on, Boudinot acknowledges the power of blood to define race and preclude the rights of citizenship, and even dares to mix this blood through an audacious appropriation of the Christian Bible. The lecturer next shrinks the distance of Native Americans as well as whites from their "ancient" savage behavior, in a way that might even acknowledge the noble and primitive roots of Europeans. Finally, in asserting a common Christian humanity, Boudinot claims a shared, "equal" future to situate the indigenous nation on a coeval timeline. Anticipating new theories of human evolution such as those of Lewis Henry Morgan, ethnologist and author of *Ancient Society* (1877), Boudinot reminds listeners to keep faith in the inexorable advancement of savage people through barbarism and into civilization.

Other Cherokee writers, such as John Ridge, were less ingratiating in their requests for funding to support the advancement of Cherokees into western culture. In 1822 he delivered an address to the Circular Church in Charleston. Like Boudinot, Ridge organized his address to affirm the desire and success of the civilizing mission. But he veers from his cousin when he challenges the "civilized man" for his primitivism: "It is said by some that there is more real enjoyment predominant in the savage than in the civilized man. But I question who would renounce the privileges of polished society for a wild abode in the wilderness. Will anyone believe that an Indian who walks solitary in the mountains, exposed to cold and hunger, or to the attacks of wild beasts, actually possesses undisturbed contentment superior to a learned gentleman who has every possible comfort at home?"

Though Cherokee writers at times draw on a romantic idealism that invites readers to sympathize with their cause, at other times authors are better served to reject such idealism, here in the image of the Noble Savage. Ridge angrily refuses the misguided sentiment that values Natural Man as uncorrupted, and that conveniently supports removal to save this Noble Savage by preserving his purity in the west. In reimagining man in the wilderness he exposes the hypocrisy of primitivism. Ridge trades the Noble Savage for modern comforts and refinement. No apologies.

But by far the Cherokees' most effective medium for their international project was the *Cherokee Phoenix*. Each issue placed lasting traditions and changing industry and politics in columns next to North American and world events both in Cherokee and in English for an international readership. With the help of Worcester, Boudinot printed official legislation passed by the Cherokee National Council, notices of weddings, school examinations, meetings of temperance societies, and Christian scripture and hymns to advertise the accomplishments of his people. The *Cherokee Phoenix* invited the syndication of news, poetry, and official statements from the United States and abroad. On its pages readers found the words of North American leaders from Jackson and Webster to John Calhoun, Lewis Cass, Sam Houston, and Davy Crockett together with the writings of Washington Irving, Jane Johnston Schoolcraft, Black Hawk, Red Jacket, and Peter Jones. Here is a statement from the *Hartford Times* concerning the imprisonment of William Apess:

> The Rev. Mr. Apess, the missionary among the Mashpee Indians, in Massachusetts, has been sentenced to thirty days imprisonment, and ordered to recognize with one surety to keep the peace, for his attempting to establish the Independence of the poor Indians. It is probable that the missionaries to the Cherokees will get up a great excitement against this tyrannical and oppressive act of the government of Massachusetts. They at least ought to do this to be consistent.

In entering this global print culture an international readership discovers the cause of the Mashpee, and North Americans throughout the eastern continent are called to respond. Though serving the Native national cause, nineteenth-century Native American writers gained legitimacy and opposed removal by promoting the humanity they shared with members of other indigenous and settler nations.

Chapter 4

From artifact to intellectual

In Washington, DC, in the 1830s, Native American diplomats in suits and ties bustled about town. Seneca leader Red Jacket was on a lecture tour and Cherokee Principal Chief John Ross negotiated Indian removal policies. Yet around this same time a Native American man arrived in buckskin, beads, and feathers to stand on balconies and stare menacingly at the capital's crowds. He was not to be feared, however, for in April and May 1833 he traveled as a federal prisoner on a forced tour throughout the East.

His name was Ma-ka-tai-me-she-kia-kaik or Black Sparrow Hawk, more commonly called Black Hawk. He had lost the Black Hawk War and President Andrew Jackson ordered him to Washington, but he apparently served as such an image of the frontier that the writer Washington Irving and painters George Catlin and Robert Sully also visited him after his capture and delayed his departure. Together with seven other members of his nation, Black Hawk traveled under military escort by steamship up the Ohio River to Wheeling, in what was then Virginia, where his entourage took the Cumberland Road to the capital of the United States.

Two days after arriving, Black Hawk stood before the president, who asked why he dared defy the United States. Black Hawk

MA - KA - TAI - ME - SHE - KIA - KIAH
BLACK HAWK A SAUKIE BRAVE

6. In April and May 1833, Black Hawk was shackled and summoned to Washington to stand before President Jackson. After imprisonment and during a tour of eastern cities, he sat for a portrait by Charles Bird King, which joined the gallery of famous chiefs housed in the Department of War.

Native American Literature

replied at length but Jackson appeared uninterested. Next the president ordered the Sauk prisoners to Fort Monroe in Virginia, where they languished for another five weeks. Then the men toured eastern cities, where they saw plays and visited the Philadelphia waterworks, the U.S. Mint, a local prison, the New York arsenal, a fireworks display, and even a hot air balloon from which the ballooner declared Black Hawk a hero in the image of those of the American Revolution. The Sauk war leader obliged his public by sporting a buffalo headdress at a formal dance in Philadelphia and, above all, by announcing his defeat and subsequent wish to befriend the whites.

In an ironic example of the era's complicated ethnic sentiments, in Baltimore the president and Black Hawk attended the same performance of a play called *Jim Crow*, probably a minstrel show in which white actors in black face makeup performed the antics of foolish but happy slaves. Citizens arrived to see Black Hawk as much as they did to see the commander in chief, or perhaps as much as to view the image of happy slaves. In fact, Jackson became frustrated in finding Black Hawk a celebrity whose presence created not support for removal policy but rather sympathy for Native Americans, and so Jackson cut the tour short and sent the Sauk villains home.

The Black Hawk War of 1832 was the last U.S. attack on Native people east of the Mississippi River. In that war future government leaders Abraham Lincoln, Zachary Taylor, Winfield Scott, and Jefferson Davis proved themselves as "Indian fighters" worthy of federal office. Most of all, the war enabled Andrew Jackson to demonstrate Indian removal as a workable policy. As in many removal-era conflicts, a dishonorable treaty lay behind this allied Sauk and Fox battle with local militia in Illinois and Wisconsin. In 1804 General William Henry Harrison arranged with an unauthorized group of Sauks to buy their ancestral lands between the Illinois and Mississippi Rivers. Sauks remained on the land until about 1830 when the United States finally surveyed and began to sell the land. While most Sauks found resistance futile and agreed to resettle west of the Mississippi, Black Hawk and his followers vowed to remain in their homes as they had for more than a century, returning in April 1832. After a series of skirmishes, the U.S. militia cornered Black Hawk's band along the Mississippi River near Bad Axe, Wisconsin, where they killed or captured most of the group. In what was not actually a war but a massacre, the United States lost five men.

On his surrender Black Hawk hoped to set the record straight. Indian agency interpreter Antoine LeClaire and newspaperman John B. Patterson helped publish the *Life of Black Hawk* (1833) in an effort to relate "the *causes* that had impelled him to act as he had done, and the *principles* by which he is governed." Though some question its authenticity, statements throughout Black Hawk's *Life* suggest strongly that the three men communicated his life narrative as clearly as possible. Indeed, in an era when North America justified its cupidity for indigenous lands with views of irredeemable Indian savagery, Patterson's advertisement for the book describes Black Hawk as "a Hero who has lately taken such high rank among the distinguished individuals of America." Throughout his narrative the Sauk "hero" insists on the truth of his presence as an eyewitness to the multiple injustices and atrocities committed against his nation, and he refuses to narrate events that he himself did not experience.

The autobiography includes Sauk origin stories and customs, and it delivers a powerful counternarrative of U.S. entitlement to indigenous lands during the clamor for Indian removal. Black Hawk is still traumatized by the memory of the appalling theft of his ancestral place: "to be driven from our village and hunting grounds, and not even permitted to visit the graves of our forefathers, our relations, and friends! This hardship is not known to the whites." He reveals a deep sense of history, recorded in and sanctified by the homeland itself. Such ties to irreplaceable indigenous lands render Indian removal not only unworkable but also unethical, he affirms.

Black Hawk next presents his vision of *reason* in challenging western notions of property. "My reason," he argues, "teaches me that land cannot be sold. The Great Spirit gave it to his children to live upon, and cultivate as far as is necessary for their subsistence; and so long as they occupy and cultivate it, they have the right to the soil—but if they voluntarily leave it, then any other people have the right to settle upon it. Nothing can be sold but such things as can be carried away." In relying on reason to present his claim, Black Hawk contradicts common conclusions about the incapacity of Indians to think or govern; indeed, he couples reason with governance in his narrative. Moreover, in providing his critique of western views on property, Black Hawk invites North American readers to acknowledge the invention of their purportedly God-sanctioned expansion. Despite the success of *Life of Black Hawk*, almost all Native American autobiographies do not appear until the twentieth century.

Other histories, other travels

The Black Hawk campaign of 1832 refined an already centuries-old pattern for European dispossession of indigenous lands. North American leaders often sought the most pliable Native community members, appointed them "chiefs," and through alcohol, bribery, intimidation, or deception compelled them to sign treaties ceding millions of acres for smaller lands with limited resources farther west. Colonial officials also did little to keep white settlers from entering these new indigenous territories or assaulting Native Americans there despite pleas from Native leaders, but they often retaliated violently when Native Americans defended their new lands. Similar histories echo throughout the so-called Indian Wars of the nineteenth century.

Meanwhile Native people continued to write. Ojibwe families who had built wealth in the fur trade often sent their children to eastern schools, from which they returned to write and lead. The Schoolcrafts were one such family. Agent to the Sault Saint Marie community, Henry Rowe Schoolcraft married into the prominent Ojibwe Johnston family. As a self-styled "Indian expert," territorial governor Lewis Cass sent an exhaustive questionnaire on Indian life to all Indian agents, and Schoolcraft asked his wife, Jane Johnston Schoolcraft, to consult elders and assemble her own "polite literature of the Chippewa." Schoolcraft drew on this collection for his own work. Unfortunately, in *Algic Researches* (1839), the first volume of Native American literature, Schoolcraft suggests that Ojibwe stories provide evidence that the Indian mind is childlike and incapable of self-government. Partially on Schoolcraft's evidence Cass argued in print and before Congress the inherent racial inferiority and inevitable demise of Native Americans.

By the middle nineteenth century American ethnology had scant interest in indigenous oral literatures, finding them often nonsensical and warranting attention merely as entertainment. Many North Americans believed that without literacy, Native Americans were without history, and without history they were without civilization. Living in these times and potentially encumbered by theories of inherent Indian difference, Ojibwe writers such as Peter Jones, George Copway, and William Warren sought to place themselves and Ojibwes in time, as conscious agents adapting to a changing world. Each man thus authored a history presenting Ojibwe people not as a vanishing race, but as a people cultivating indigenous knowledge in new circumstances. All these writers showcased the aesthetic power of Ojibwe thought and literature.

Peter Jones converted to his white father's Methodism in 1823. While fervently establishing missions he wrote *History of the Ojibway Indians* (1860). Jones openly confronts white assumptions of racial supremacy, arguing that he "cannot suppose for a moment that the Supreme Disposer has decreed…the doom of the red man." Though Jones cites its persistence as evidence of the vitality of traditional knowledge, he predicts an increasingly Christian path for Native Americans. Even though some have perceived Jones to present Native people as not "inherently different" but rather as "morally depraved," he writes at length about the value of such Ojibwe religious experiences as dreams, a fact suggesting his ambivalence about eclipsing Ojibwe ways. More importantly, throughout his *History* Jones fights for indigenous rights to self-government, albeit on Christian terms.

In 1830 Jones converted a "pious" Ojibwe student named George Copway. By 1834, as a missionary at the Saugeen mission on Lake Huron, Copway was indicted for embezzlement, sent to prison in Toronto, and expelled from the church. He overlooked this checkered past in *The Life, History, and Travels of Kah-ge-ga-gah-bowh (George Copway), a Young Indian Chief of the Ojibwa Nation, A Convert to the Christian Faith, and a Missionary to His People for Twelve Years* (1847).

Copway became a supreme self-promoter, touring to lecture and befriending Francis Parkman and Henry Wadsworth Longfellow among other ranking members of society only to become indebted and again jailed in New York. Afterward Copway travelled as an "Indian doctor," changed his name, and became a Catholic healer on Grand Island reserve in Ontario. Throughout what he calls his "crooked travels" Copway undermines the exact role of the Noble Savage that he has been asked to perform. Like Jones, in his *History* Copway argues for the advancement of Ojibwes through Christian conversion. Though Copway refers often to the Ojibwe Grand Medicine Lodge, he promotes both Christianity and literacy; like a handful of Cherokees he advocates removal to a specifically Christian Ojibwe reservation, even as he argues for the beauty and value of Ojibwe oral literature.

William Warren learned Ojibwe ceremony and language as a child, then attended boarding school in his white father's native New York. Upon return, Warren became a government interpreter in Michigan and later a territorial legislator in Minnesota. He began collecting oral literature from his elders and published them in the

Minnesota Democrat, then wrote his *History of the Ojibway Nation, Based upon Traditions and Oral Statements*. Through its anchor in oral literatures, Warren's history challenges the era's dominant modes of writing Native American history. Some argue that Warren offered this challenge precisely because, unlike Jones and Copway, he bore no ties to Christian missions. Warren felt no obligation to narrate his conversion to Christianity; instead, he delivers a scholarly study of Ojibwe stories of migrations and settlements, medicine societies and ceremonies. Throughout, Warren allows Ojibwe knowledge to correct western misrepresentations, and he proclaims Ojibwe autonomy to write their own history.

In arguments likely pointed at Henry Schoolcraft, he writes to confront the work of "transient sojourners," who "not having a full knowledge of their character and language, have obtained information through mere temporary observation—through the medium of careless and imperfect interpreters, or have taken the account of unreliable persons." In writing what he calls "the first work written from purely Indian sources," Warren finally crosses a color line in the study of Native Americans and their literatures. In 1852 he set off for New York to find a publisher and a doctor for his growing illness. Not surprisingly Warren could not find a publisher for his self-possessed work, and he died a year later at the age of twenty-eight.

George Copway toured Europe and in 1851 wrote the first full-length Native American travelogue, *Running Sketches of Men and Places*. Around this time Peter Jones's half-brother Maungwudaus undertook a similar mission, and wrote *An Account of the Chippewa Indians: Who Have Been Travelling among the Whites* (1848). Having left the church, Maungwudaus organized a touring Ojibwe dance troupe. A talented entrepreneur in the thriving Indian business, Maungwudaus toured with western painter George Catlin, though Maungwudaus's writings challenge Catlin's frequently romantic vision of the noble yet doomed Indian. Maungwudaus's narrative introduces a clever reversal: for once indigenous people "discover" Europeans and struggle to understand their strange customs.

Indigenous lives

From Indian Territory and throughout the East Native American intellectuals such as Odawa historian Andrew Blackbird, Wyandot intellectual Peter Clarke, and Cherokee journalist E. C. Boudinot wrote as Native North America moved toward the U.S. Civil War. After the war, with Congress declaring in 1871 that the United States would no longer make treaties with indigenous nations, and after the Wounded Knee Massacre in 1890, Native Americans found that they had reached the depth of national autonomy. In their final conquest of indigenous land and people, North Americans took the show on the road. At the 1893 World's Columbian Exposition in Chicago, actual Native people were displayed in dioramas as relics of the frontier past, living proof that the frontier had closed, as historian Frederick Jackson Turner announced at the fair. Some Native Americans at the exposition actively contested Turner's narrative, when, for example, Potawatomie intellectual Simon Pokagon publicly pronounced: "In behalf of my people, the American Indians, I hereby declare to you, the pale-faced race that has usurped our lands and homes, that we have no spirit to celebrate with you." This was the bitter world of Native people at the turn of the twentieth century.

By the early twentieth century ethnographers and Indian enthusiasts sought out those Native Americans who survived the Indian Wars but still had a clear memory of pre-contact life on the plains. Many Native autobiographies from this era are translated into English from indigenous languages. Readers often question the authenticity of such narratives, mediated as they are by amanuenses, translators, and editors. In some texts the European voice is minimal, in others dominant, and researchers often study archives of a particular work to disclose that intervention or collaboration. Despite these complexities readers remain fascinated with Native American autobiographies, which number in the hundreds, and Native people as well plumb these sources to hear an ancestor speak or to revive a ceremony.

In perhaps the best known Native American autobiography, *Black Elk Speaks* (1932), an aged Sioux man describes his childhood vision and lifelong failure to honor it: "But now that I can see it all as from a lonely hilltop, I know it was the story of a mighty vision given to a man too weak to use it; of a holy tree that should have flourished in a people's heart with flowers and singing birds, and now is withered; and of a people's dream that died in bloody snow." From the opening page of this life story readers empathize with this man's tragic inability to fulfill his divine gift, and the story's recorder, poet John Neihardt, no doubt employed his art to create this autobiography of one gifted man's failure to save the world. At the same time, however, by inviting such romantic readings Neihardt potentially also leads readers to believe that Sioux losses occurred as much from the failures of individuals as from military atrocity.

Within this familiar narrative frame, however, the stalwart voice of Black Elk nonetheless emerges. As a youth he travelled through Europe while performing in Buffalo Bill's Wild West show. Like Maungwudaus, Black Elk escaped confinement on a reservation by internationalizing Native culture in ways only recently recognized in Native American studies. The autobiography also delivers Black Elk's eyewitness account of the massacre at Wounded Knee: the U.S. Seventh Cavalry had surrounded a group of Sioux performing a religious rite and demanded surrender. A single shot was fired, and the soldiers swooped in among the families with Hotchkiss guns, killing their own soldiers and as many as 300 Sioux. Like Black Hawk's narrative, Black Elk's testimony counters mainstream narratives and demands justice for the dead.

Such alternative colonial histories from the other side of the frontier appear from unlikely autobiographical sources. In *Pretty*

Shield: Medicine Woman of the Crows (1932), Frank Linderman records Pretty Shield's account of life on the northern plains before and after the arrival of Europeans. The Crow matriarch details the 1876 Battle of the Little Big Horn in which the Seventh Cavalry was defeated, killed to a man, by assembled Native American groups. Relating the account of her husband, Goes-ahead, who scouted for Custer, Pretty Shield argues that Custer never made a "last stand" but was shot at the battle's beginning. Elsewhere her stories challenge western views of knowledge, as when dreams determine reality and knowledge increases from discussions with animals: "Did any of the animal-people ever talk to you. . .?" Pretty Shield then tells of a time when a mouse told her entire band to move to avoid danger, and so they did. The "'woman-mouse' gave this warning: "My friend! My friend! In four days you will be attacked by the Lacota." Though Linderman often listens in disbelief to stories about ancient giants, wolf men, talking antelope, and healing miracles, he probably transcribed Pretty Shield's words with precision, for the two conversed in the sign language that had acted as a translingual trade language across the plains for centuries. Pretty Shield's life narrative and that written by her relative, *Plenty Coup: Chief of the Crows* (1930), remain rare specimens of Indian sign-talk autobiography.

Other Native women's autobiographies such as that of Sarah Winnemucca's *Life among the Piutes: Their Wrongs and Claims* (1883) remind the North American public that Native women bear a strong history of leadership. Educated in western schools and having served as a U.S. military guide, Winnemucca toured the United States and spoke defiantly against dishonored treaties and land thefts. Her autobiography helped to establish a school and homeland for the Paiutes. Other narratives are more whimsical: in *Mountain Wolf Woman* (1961) the author describes the Winnebago traditions of selecting a husband, which involved receiving new clothes from his sisters and gathering lily roots—in waist deep water with one's feet.

In 1879 the U.S. federal government intensified its efforts to westernize Native Americans with the opening of Carlisle Indian Industrial School in Pennsylvania. For more than a century some North Americans believed that Native people could be "civilized"— or later, "assimilated" into the workforce—if only their cultures were destroyed and their children forcibly removed from their homes and reprogrammed. Former army captain Richard Pratt, who offered his infamous motto, "Kill the Indian, Save the Man," led the Carlisle school. Workers in a network of Indian boarding and residential schools throughout North America beat Native American children for speaking their languages, sexually abused them, exposed them to diseases, and placed them behind bars. Thousands died and were buried in school cemeteries, their parents sometimes never knowing their children's fate.

In *My People the Sioux* (1928) Luther Standing Bear, a member of Carlisle's first class, describes how he received his name: "[O]ur interpreter came into the room and said, 'Do you see all these marks on the blackboard? Well, each word is a white man's name. They are going to give each one of you one of these names by which you will hereafter be known.' None of the names were read or explained to us, so of course we did not know the sound or meaning of any of them." This random act of renaming Native children as white men and women comes to stand for the boarding school mission, which demanded the utter destruction of indigenous culture and the remaking of Native Americans into farm and factory laborers.

Elsewhere in works such as in Francis La Flesche's *Middle Five* (1900) the boarding school is also recalled with tender humor. Yet the undercurrent of pain resurfaces, as in Standing Bear's *Land of the Spotted Eagle* (1933). Here Standing Bear declares the uselessness of divesting Native people of culture on reservations "where the young are unfitted for tribal life and untrained for the world of white man's affairs except to hold an occasional job!" Instead, Standing Bear pleas for colonial governments to "give back to Indian youth all, everything in their heritage that belongs to them and augment it with the best in the modern schools." Finally he returns to his Sioux roots, arguing that the refusal of Native Americans to relinquish "the Indian blanket" and other traditions will ultimately save them from the rapacity of North American settler colonialism. In *From the Deep Woods to Civilization* (1916), Charles Eastman charts his youth hunting far from European settlements, his entrance into western schools, and his eventual practice as a physician at the Pine Ridge Agency, where he ministered to victims of the 1890 Wounded Knee massacre. That experience galvanized his conclusion that there was more savagery in western civilization than in Native communities, and that capitalism was ultimately opposed to Christianity. After writing a dozen books, Eastman "went back to the blanket" and returned to his Dakota woods. In multiple later autobiographies and memoirs, Native Americans finally give full voice to the deplorable injustice of the residential and boarding schools.

Native autobiographies sometimes surprise readers with their social subversions. In *Crashing Thunder* (1926), the Winnebago author tells how in his youth he sought desperately for a vision to guide his life. As instructed by his father he fasted for four days. On the fifth morning, he writes: "I told my elder brother that I had been blessed by the spirits and that I was going home to eat. I was not speaking the truth. I was hungry." Throughout his life Crashing Thunder lies, cheats, and tricks women into favors. Anthropologist Paul Radin lauds this story of a true "rake's progress," but evidence shows that the recorder took great license in creating that character, going as far as changing the author's name. In these and seemingly countless Native American autobiographies we gain at least a glimpse into indigenous patterns of living, ways of knowing, and verbal art. The genre fueled the revitalization of indigenous nations in the 1960s and 1970s, when, after decades of silence, authors recorded colonial oppression and resistance. In *Halfbreed* (1978), Maria Campbell recalls poverty in a Metis family, while later, in *Interior*

Landscapes (1990), Gerald Vizenor recounts the place of Anishinaabe story in his urban tale of abandonment and community belonging.

Writing reform

In 1887 Congress passed the General Allotment Act, which divided communally held Indian lands into individually owned and taxable parcels, with the largest lots given to usually male "heads of families." After this redistribution, all "surplus" lands were made available to non-Native settlers. By 1932 allotment had led to the loss of 26 million acres, or two-thirds of all indigenous lands. Many Native American writers were aware of allotment's insidious theft of lands as well as its "mighty pulverizing engine to break up the tribal mass," as Theodore Roosevelt put it.

Especially in Indian Territory newspapers served as the locus of resistance. In 1902 a young Creek man named Alexander Posey began satirizing claims by white legislators that they knew what was best for Native Americans, including allotment, railroads, and Oklahoma statehood. Posey invented a "red English" dialect that became a nationally syndicated sensation. Here for instance his persona "Stootee" plays the Injun fool: "One man come my house lass week en tell me: 'Stoo-tee, I want make it town site you places....' I ask him, that man, what it is he call it ton sites. I got it 'fo sites' en 'hine sites' on my guns, but I dont know what tis, 'ton sites.'" Stootee suggests here that guns serve Native people better than a clear understanding of colonial language or property division. Cherokee intellectuals DeWitt Clinton Duncan and William Eubanks employed the newspapers to express disagreement on allotment, but by 1922 Native American journalism discovered one of the most famous Native people in the world—Will Rogers. His humor asserted Native presence and disclosed settler colonialism: "My ancestors didn't come over on the *Mayflower*—they met the boat."

In an era of reform, from around 1890 to 1934, Native and non-Native activists sought legislation to "uplift" the Indian, though the goals of reformers often conflicted, especially once Native Americans represented themselves in the movement. Natives and whites actively collaborated through the Society of American Indians (SAI) to influence federal Indian policy. The Society's Native people made their primary cause United States citizenship, which they belatedly received with the 1924 birthright citizenship act for Native Americans. SAI sociologist Fayette McKenzie urged Native people to enter previously exclusionary public discussions on the future of the Indian.

In his letter of invitation, he explained the SAI's challenge: "The chief reason we continue to have an Indian problem is because the public generally does not believe that the Indian is capable of education, culture, or high morality." McKenzie wished to seize the moment when the United States had finally detribalized and educated its first classes of Native Americans to western standards. Members of the SAI, such as Seneca archaeologist Arthur C. Parker, Apache physician Carlos Montezuma, Sioux musicologist Zitkala-Ša, Sioux physician Charles Eastman, Arapahoe minister Sherman Coolidge, Cherokee novelist John Oskison, and Omaha anthropologist Francis LaFlesche, were thus handpicked for inclusion among the western-educated Native Americans of the early twentieth century. With non-Native members they convened annually to plan the "adjustment" of Native Americans to new realities and to press for the grant of U.S. citizenship to Native Americans. The society's journal, which included essays, fiction, and poetry, became the conduit for dispensing their message to the mainstream public.

The SAI labored to negotiate tangled views of race. While many reformers, such as Charles Harvey, flatly declared the inevitable, natural demise of Native Americans, others, such as Fayette McKenzie, Richard Pratt, Lyman Abbot, and James McLaughlin, viewed the so-called Indian problem as "sink or swim": to survive Native people must jettison their cultures and assimilate fully into North American society. Of course in either case indigenous cultures would vanish. Of the many philanthropic organizations working with the SAI to save the Indian, such as the Lake Mohonk Friends of the Indian, most agreed on enforced assimilation of Native Americans.

Members of the SAI devised a compromise to this demand for the destruction of tribal tradition and rapid assumption of European ways. Anthropologist Frank Speck suggested that Native people should maintain their customs to contribute to the art and culture of the United States. So Arthur Parker presented his "sane middle ground" to the sink or swim policy wherein "the Indian of America may wear his own style of swimming suit and use his own special swimming stroke. He will progress faster and keep afloat by doing so." Parker consistently presented his "adjustment policy" as a process in which Native Americans pursue a parallel yet distinct path toward the goals of universal humanity to "adjust himself to modern conditions." Oskison, on the other hand, describes a "new Indian" who lives off the reservation and contributes to the U.S. economy, a "modern Indian" who has left behind the "dirty beggar" created by the reservation system. Oskison celebrates this "new man" as being "Indian only in blood and traditions."

This reality characterized the troubling case of Native political activity in the early twentieth century. While Arthur Parker, as editor of the SAI journal from 1913 to 1918, clearly is representative of the most pervasive, accommodating voice in the society, others such as Carlos Montezuma were not content to accept the SAI's often idealistic, moderate appeals to government officials for citizenship. Orphaned, adopted by North Americans, and living in urban Chicago, Montezuma abhorred the reservation as a "demoralizing prison" and called for its destruction, as well that of the entire Bureau of Indian Affairs. Increasingly strident in his views, Montezuma became a threat to the affiliation of the SAI with other organizations, and Parker and Zitkala-Ša worked to calm him down. Zitkala-Ša lists other differences within the SAI. Unlike Montezuma, who was mentored by and admired Pratt, Zitkala-Ša disliked Pratt, for whom she had taught at Carlisle, and rails against reform in her short story "The Soft-Hearted Sioux." Though involved in the SAI, Charles Eastman shied away from direct political discussions; instead, he produced idealized accounts of pre-reservation life in which the Indian body and religion were harmoniously related. With his more aesthetic interests Eastman nonetheless balanced the movement.

Most hostile to the spirit of reform was Luther Standing Bear, who announced that the Indian could survive only by refusing assimilation. Writing after the disbandment of the SAI, Standing Bear declared the reform era a disaster, one that left young Native Americans robbed of their lands, languages, and customs, unable to speak with elders, and poor imitators of North Americans. Like Zitkala-Ša, Standing Bear in the 1930s looked to his reservation community and saw no improvements on the part of the SAI programs, but only greater poverty consequent to empty idealism. While the SAI facilitated public discussion, it derived from a closely guarded forum of Native elites, as Parker himself had wished. The Society of American Indians envisioned itself a "Mohonk by Indians," and the Mohonk Conference's pet project was the allotment of indigenous lands. Members of the SAI also supported the outlawing of indigenous religions such as the peyotist Native American Church, and the SAI generally supported the boarding school system. Even if it was a failure or served as a force of destruction, the Society of American Indians nonetheless helped to save Native American writers for the twentieth century, scattering the cultural seeds for later Native literary flourishing.

Chapter 5
Native American literary studies

On November 9, 1969, a young Native American student dove from a borrowed sailboat into the frigid waters of San Francisco Bay and swam 250 yards against swift currents to reclaim Alcatraz Island as indigenous land. A Mohawk man from the St. Regis Reservation in upstate New York, Richard Oakes had migrated to San Francisco to join a community of Native people "relocated" to urban areas during the 1950s era of federal tribal termination. By the 1960s generations of Native Americans in the Bay area had grown restless about their displacement and poverty, and young people responded by organizing across Native groups and raising their voices in public protest. While attending San Francisco State College, Oakes gathered with other students to sharpen this vision of renewal for indigenous North America. The San Francisco State College group soon reached out to bring its dream of change to Native American student organizations at UC Berkeley and UCLA. The Red Power movement had begun among Native students. Native American writers too imagined a new narrative for Turtle Island, neither by longing for an impossibly timeless past nor by disconnecting the stories of Native Americans from the political realities of their lives. Instead the era's authors worked better to interpret a colonized world and to offer this new knowledge to empower the people.

Following the occupation of Alcatraz in 1969, a decade-long flurry of events would define the Red Power era: the 1972 march on Washington for the Trail of Broken Treaties; the 1973 takeover of Wounded Knee; the 1975 intervention of the American Indian Movement on the Pine Ridge reservation; the 1978 Longest Walk on Washington to reenact the displacement of Native peoples from their homelands. Between these touchstone events, elders, faith keepers, students, scholars, and activists organized dozens of occupations of stolen indigenous territories, staged takeovers of corrupt Bureau of Indian Affairs (BIA) offices, and filed multiple legal claims demanding the return of stolen lands and property, as well as compensation for centuries of cultural destruction.

Meanwhile Native American students brought their visions of justice to college campuses to create what they began to describe as

7. Native Americans occupy Alcatraz Island in 1969. The graffiti on the prison's water tower reads in red: "Peace and Freedom. Welcome. Home of the Free. Indian Land."

"Native American Studies." Pressuring universities to accept a more diverse student body, Native scholars demanded that universities allow the production of knowledge by and for Native Americans. Sioux scholar Elizabeth Cook-Lynn recalls participating in this moment: "[We asserted] that Indians were not just the inheritors of trauma but were also the heirs to vast legacies of knowledge about this continent and the universe that had been ignored in the larger picture of European invasion and education."

Antiquarians and Indian salvage

To succeed, Native American Studies had to tear free of the "salvage anthropology" that shaped the European study of indigenous people from the first moments of contact. As early as 1527 when Cabeza de Vaca wandered around Texas and published his detailed account of Native Americans, such explorers have sought to understand the worlds of indigenous peoples, but they did so usually in ethnocentric terms, and through the eyes of the conquerors. The Old World voraciously consumed proto-anthropological accounts, numbering Native people of the Americas among the most studied people in the world. John White thus entered an already engrained tradition when he arrived with the 1585 Roanoke Colony of North Carolina and created the first known European depictions of Native Americans in North America, and by 1608 to aid his trade and mining mission John Smith began to publish his account of Native people in Virginia. In 1620 William Bradford began his record of Plymouth wherein he includes careful study of the colony's indigenous neighbors with an eye toward converting them to Christianity.

By the eighteenth century North American settlers began to make Native Americans the focus of their studies, with intellectuals such as Cadwallader Colden writing his *History of the Five Indian Nations* (1727) and James Adair his *History of the American Indians* (1775). In 1791 William Bartram published on his extensive travels in the indigenous Southeast. One of the best-known antiquarians was Thomas Jefferson, who, in his *Notes on the State of Virginia* (1785), described excavating and examining Native American burial remains in earthen monuments on his estate. An early member of the American Antiquarian Society established in 1812 and peopled by many American founders, Jefferson discussed the necessity of antiquarians to study, collect, and catalogue, that is, salvage, the ancient Adena and Hopewell monuments on the Ohio River before settlers plowed them under.

Of course the question of whether Europeans truly could understand the histories of these indigenous peoples, let alone whether they had the right to desecrate Native American burials, did not arise. Long before their arrival in the Americas, Europeans had invented the interdependent concepts of savagism and civilization. Civilization, in a manner, needed savagery to affirm its superiority. For this reason the savage had to remain, if only in memory. Native people thus existed as relics who demanded collection. In fact, like many North Americans, Jefferson believed not only that contemporaneous Native Americans bore no relationship to America's ancient earthworks, but also that his era's savage Indians had actually exterminated the continent's ancient, advanced race of "moundbuilders."

Along with the concept of savagism, the idea of the Vanishing Indian drove the collection and study of Native objects and peoples. As a discovered remnant of unchanging, primitive man, the Indian would melt before the tide of American progress. He would leave the land to civilized people, who evolved in time, possessing both a history and the intellectual means to record it. North Americans who crossed the frontier, such as Superintendent of Indian Affairs Thomas McKenney, or Michigan territorial governor Lewis Cass, or painter and author George Catlin, returned East with what they considered to be records of disappearing Indians. In 1832 antiquarian Samuel Drake published his *Indian Biography*. From his bookstore or "Institute of Miscellaneous Literature," Drake sold tickets to William Apess's performance of *Eulogy on King Philip*, which drew heavily on Drake's history of indigenous New England. Drake's bookstore attracted editors of magazines on Indian antiquities such as Jared Sparks, who published Cass's essays supporting Indian removal by arguing that indigenous people's languages lacked the complexity to support civilized thought.

By the 1870s, when the United States had removed most eastern Native nations to the West and established the reservation system, the new Bureau of Ethnology had categorized the resulting collection of Native American objects and oral literatures. In 1879 an act of congress established the Bureau of American Ethnology to transfer governmental and cultural materials relating to Native people from the Interior Department to the Smithsonian Institution. But its founding director, John Wesley Powell, also envisioned the bureau as the vessel to support a burgeoning new field of anthropology.

While the Smithsonian requested that military officers gather Native American bodily remains and cultural materials from the battlefield, dozens of scholars conducted fieldwork by living near or in Native communities, where they sought "informants" for their studies. Into the early twentieth century the bureau's staff comprised some of the best-known ethnologists in the field's beginnings, such as Frank Cushing and James Mooney, and supported the research of other scholars, such as Franz Boas, Frances Densmore, Washington Matthews, and Paul Radin. Such researchers translated and recorded songs, ritual dramas, and narratives including epics, legends, and stories. Like their informally trained predecessors, these early anthropologists tended to assume that European culture was superior and evolving toward progress in a pattern that would eventually overwhelm inferior, static indigenous cultures. From this vantage the Native American informant was performing the life and mindset of a previous evolutionary stage of humankind, and the anthropologist could simply record this performance. But much was lost in translation. James Mooney recorded the stories of his Cherokee informants, who sang songs central to the ancient narratives. He did not view the songs as integral to the stories, however, and so elected not to include them.

Most privileged were those Native people who in the minds of North Americans exuded the nascent virtues of humanity. This Noble Savage lived close to nature and displayed courage, generosity, and eloquence. He was usually male and a great, though defeated, warrior. Other recorders such as Paul Radin sought out his opposite, the Ignoble Savage. Radin's Indian "rogue" stole, lied, and tricked women into marriage. Radin purchased the confidence of his impoverished informant, who was probably reluctant to disappoint his benefactor, and so

8. On one of his frequent trips to Washington as a Blackfoot representative, in 1916 Mountain Chief agreed to demonstrate the ethnographic process for photographers. Here, he interprets a song in plains Indian sign language for the ethnologist Frances Densmore, who sought to preserve Native American music.

embellished his tale to please him. Then Radin copiously altered his informant's story to please his editor. Bearing this troubled, colonized history, anthropology came to be viewed as predatory by mid-twentieth-century Native Americans. By the late 1960s Native activists confronted archeologists digging without full permission on indigenous lands, asking them if it would be acceptable for Native Americans to dig in Arlington, the U.S. national cemetery.

Red Power led Native scholars to announce that the study of a people will improve when those people themselves contribute to that study. More importantly, the scholars accomplished an imaginative shift in self-conception: Native Americans are not helpless victims of colonial devastation; rather, they are the shrewd protectors of indigenous thought. Like the Red Power activists on Alcatraz, these Native intellectuals underwent a moment of self-realization. Whereas mainstream academics had long held that Native Americans were spiraling in decline, Native intellectuals studied and publicized the fact that Native people still practiced the old ways and continually invented new ones—on Alcatraz, on reservations, in cities, in universities. If Native Americans were hopelessly conquered, how could they be sharing traditional knowledge at Princeton? At the close of the decade, Native scholars and organizers built from the ground up a process-oriented view of indigenous knowledge and a vision of cultural renewal to inform the criticism, politics, and art of Native America.

A Native American emergence

In the late 1840s the pioneering anthropologist Lewis Henry Morgan sought the knowledge of the Parker siblings on the Tonawanda Seneca reservation to write what became *League of the Iroquois* (1851). Ely S. Parker was Morgan's primary informant, and some scholars even believe that he should be credited as co-author. Parker was educated in the boarding schools, and his surviving papers show that he studied the rhetoric of William Apess. While other early Native writers, such as Elias Boudinot, were aware of Apess, Parker may be one of the earliest Native scholars to study indigenous writings. And for a rhetorical model Parker could not do better than Apess.

As the first Native American Commissioner of Indian Affairs, Ely Parker extended Apess's example to write on Native issues, and by the early twentieth century his great nephew Arthur C. Parker, eventual head of the Society of American Indians (SAI), became an archaeologist at the New York State Museum and the foremost authority on Iroquois culture and history, writing *The Code of Handsome Lake* (1913) and *The Constitution of the Five Nations* (1916), among many other publications. The new century saw a number of other Native American scholars trained in archaeology and anthropology, such as Omaha ethnologist Francis La Flesche, who wrote one of the most thorough ethnographies on Osages; linguist J. N. B. Hewitt, who was Tuscarora; and anthropologist Ella Deloria, a Sioux woman.

In their hard-won positions of ethnographic authority, these Native scholars signaled a shift in age-old colonial relations of power, and Native Americans slowly gained some measure of control over the assembly and study of indigenous culture and art. Not surprisingly, these earlier Native scholars found empowering models in oral literature. For instance, Charles Eastman describes the importance of a Sioux child's study to perform with precision their oral literature: "the household became his audience, by which he was alternately criticized or applauded." Luther Standing Bear declares the depth and density of Sioux oral literature: "These stories were the libraries of our people."

Later, as Red Power organizers took over indigenous lands, so Native American scholars reclaimed the study of Native literature. Like his predecessors Eastman and Standing Bear, N. Scott Momaday saw the capacity of indigenous oral literatures to serve contemporary Native American lives, even to inform a written literature, imploring Native writers to imagine their place in an ancient ancestral line of storytellers. For centuries language itself lay at the heart of Native American humanity: "Man has consummate being in language," writes Momaday. This Man Made of Words goes on to share a Kiowa story from his childhood to express the crucial role of story in indigenous societies. "The Arrowmaker" describes mastery of language as key to a people's survival. Long ago a wife and husband sat in their lodge, the man making arrows by the firelight. Soon the man noticed that someone was peering in through a seam in the lodge skin. He told his wife, "Someone is standing outside. Do not be afraid. Let us talk easily, as of ordinary things." The man pretended to test an arrow in his drawn bow, taking aim in different directions, while he talked as if to his wife. But this is what he said: "I know that you are there on the outside, for I can feel your eyes upon me. If you are Kiowa, you will understand what I am saying, and you will speak your name." There was no answer, so the man continued to point the arrow around, until training it on his enemy. He released the arrow and it pierced the enemy's heart.

In his analysis of this single story Momaday models for his audience an oral literature's ability to signify in multiple ways, from its purposes and meanings to its forms and aesthetic ideals. The tale, he explains, had been told to him since childhood, and through the years he has often interpreted it differently. In this manner Momaday reminds us that we and our literatures continue to grow together, always constituting and reconstituting one another. We must honor the ultimate mystery in story, the author suggests. "The Arrowmaker" lures us to consider the singular power of the word. Here we must face the necessity and stakes of language in the very decision to sustain or take life. With a simple declaration the man gambles everything and wins, in part because he has shown himself to be deft with language, unlike his mute and fallen enemy. Momaday here offers a few aesthetic ideals as well. The arrowmaker is nameless and "unlettered," and he enlists the most basic, honest language: "Let us talk easy, as of ordinary things." "The Arrowmaker" above all calls on Native American writers to imagine the supreme risk and thus responsibility in the holy task of language, story, and literature to restore cosmic order and community well-being.

In other early critical writings Momaday asks us to meditate on ancient pictures preserved on rocks throughout North America, which display the deep mystery of indigenous language. Such depictions, he declares, do not display the mere characters of writing, but more; they celebrate a people's culture. They are literature. In fact North American literature began when the first person looked to the land and felt compelled to express her response in language. In tying Native American literature to community and, here, to land, Momaday articulates ways to value and appreciate Native literature—he offers an indigenous criticism.

By 1979 Native American intellectuals collaborated to publish *The Remembered Earth*, a body of creative and critical writing seeking to build this indigenous literary thought. The collection owes its title to Momaday's statement: "Once in his life a man ought to concentrate his mind upon the remembered earth, I believe. He ought to give himself up to a particular landscape in his experience, to look at it from as many angles as he can, to wonder about it, to dwell upon it." Here the author prescribes a behavior, even an ethic, through which to value Native American land. In inviting this kind of contemplation, Momaday acknowledges that some Native people may have lost that relationship or, even if they do know their ancestral land, that relationship nevertheless can be improved through an actively pursued, deepening experience with the remembered earth. Momaday thus offers a model of Native American identity and literature as an evolving process founded in speculation and adaptation.

In this same collection the Laguna and Sioux writer Paula Gunn Allen delivers a rebuttal to Momaday. In "Iyani: It Goes This Way,"

Allen rejects Momaday's portrayal of indigenous land relationships and, by extension, his views on Native American culture and literature. She writes:

> We are the land. To the best of my understanding, that is the fundamental idea embedded in Native American life and culture in the Southwest. More than remembered, the Earth is the mind of the people as we are the mind of the earth. The land is not really the place (separate from ourselves) where we act out the drama of our isolate destinies. It is not a means of survival, a setting for our affairs, a resource on which we draw in order to keep our own act functioning.

In this unflinching declaration Allen challenges those Native Americans like Momaday who imagine that the land may be known through a relationship mediated by experience, the senses, or history. Indeed, such musing to Allen is ultimately self-serving of "our own act" and therefore individualist in the most western and colonizing sense. Instead, she affirms: "the Earth is, in a very real sense, the same as our self (or selves), and it is this primary point that is made in the fiction and poetry of Native American writers." To Allen, free-ranging thought of the kind Momaday invites is not necessary for those Native writers who already know the land. Also this self-absorbed contemplation might come at the expense of stewardship in actual indigenous communities.

In a later essay Allen intensifies this perspective as "a solid, impregnable, and ineradicable orientation toward a spirit-formed view of the universe, which provides an internal structure to both our consciousness and our art, ... [and is] shared by all members of tribal psychic reality." In delivering this explicit definition of a Native American perspective, Allen gives desiring Native writers and readers a strong statement on the secure state of indigenous consciousness.

As Native American literary studies further emerged in the 1980s Momaday and Allen became central voices in a growing body of

Native criticism. While the two display a good deal of complexity on many issues, on those outlined above they differ rather starkly, and even prefigure the shape of conversations in the field as they continue into the present. And these cultural debates ultimately inform literary debates. As Momaday suggests, Native American culture as well as its literature "should" grow through study or contemplation. Such an openly speculative position on indigenous knowledge recognizes the reality of cultural loss, on the one hand, and the possibility of its recovery, on the other. From Momaday's view there is an openness to the world and the place of Native peoples in it. Allen, by contrast, affirms the stability of indigenous life as intact and thriving, and often against western culture, whose people have misinterpreted Native people and thought for centuries. Momaday imagines the "process" of Native American becoming; Allen defines the "state" of indigenous life as more or less enduring, and often in opposition to settler colonies.

Into the 1990s and still today Native American scholars seek to claim more autonomy for indigenous nations and the literature that grows from them, but their means at times differ like Momaday and Allen. Choctaw intellectual Louis Owens's *Other Destinies* (1992) affirms the process of cultural exchange in colonial contacts as figured in the multiheritage "mixedblood." But in *Tribal Secrets* (1995) Osage critic Robert Warrior calls for "intellectual sovereignty" through which to build a criticism primarily from Native sources, while in *Red on Red* (1999) Creek researcher Craig Womack delivers his clarion for "literary separatism." More recently scholars argue that such Native American nationalism comes at the expense of indigenous feminism and hemispheric vision, such as in Yup'ik intellectual Shari Huhndorf's *Mapping the Americas* (2009). So swings the critical narrative. While no Native thinker denies the need for Native American freedom, they disagree on the measure it can or should be gained in connection with other nations, especially settler nations and peoples.

The Native American burden

In *Word Arrows* (1978), the Anishinaabe writer Gerald Vizenor recognizes the importance of Momaday's formative talk at the First Convocation of American Indian Scholars in 1970. In fact Vizenor combines the personification of the Man Made of Words with the Arrowmaker to create "word arrows," an early neologism honoring the power of indigenous story to defend Native American communities from hegemony. Vizenor offers a personal story in the same vein. A Native couple sat in his office at a community center, the man's face wearing a "powerful sense of personal doom." The woman was visibly homeless, intoxicated, and "ancient from abuse." The man began to blame white people and racism for all his misfortunes, including alcoholism. Vizenor replied: "You need white people, more than they need you now to blame for your problems.... You need them to keep you the way you are so you can moan in self-pity." Just then the woman pointed to the door and, in her confusion, asked the men to stand for the powwow grand entry—then broke into song. On completing an honor song she began to cry and "through her singing she became sober, her dark eyes were clear." Invoking Momaday, Vizenor recognizes in this woman the force of oral literature to awaken life and order the world.

Vizenor tackles the problem of internalized colonialism. The Native American man above relied on white oppression for self-pity. Vizenor calls such attachments "terminal creeds." Pursuing this "victimry" throughout his critical and fictional writings, Vizenor has invented a vast satirical world of Native people who are "victims of their own narcissism," as well as those who reject terminal creeds to become "postindians." At every turn Vizenor denounces tragic, debilitating reactions in Native American literature, and he celebrates the humorous, life-affirming replies of oral literature to North American colonialism.

Though the notion of terminal creeds helped found Native literary studies, the literature still often remains troubled by the image of the Vanishing Indian as well as encumbered by tragic literary themes and plots. Far too often in Native American literature, particularly novel, Native protagonists get drunk and in self-hatred self-destruct, leaping off bridges or cliff sides. While alcoholism and suicide rates remain highest in indigenous communities, Native American authors run a risk in providing a mainstream readership with this portrait of Native self-destruction. For too many North American readers the unacknowledged Vanishing Indian legacy remains, only now Native Americans do not melt into the land (as in Walt Whitman's fantasy) but quietly shoot themselves. For Native writers the impossible literary challenge lies in having to write for two often competing audiences, one wishing to understand and heal an often troubled social world, another often desiring to consume negative stereotypes to satisfy the colonial narrative of providential indigenous demise.

Native American literature often responds to colonial narratives tragicomically. In Blackfeet and Gros Ventre writer James Welch's novel *Winter in the Blood* (1974), a nameless narrator discloses a mystery in his family's oral history, that his grandparents had a defiant commitment to one another during conquest and famine. This hopeful vision, however, is complicated by an irreverent narrator, surreal dreams, and black humor, as at his grandmother's funeral:

> The hole was too short, but we didn't discover this until we had the coffin halfway down. One end went down easily enough, but the other struck against the wall. Teresa wanted us to take it out because she was sure that it was the head that was lower than the feet. Lame Bull lowered himself into the grave and jumped up and down on the high end. It went down a bit more, enough to look respectable. Teresa didn't say anything, so he leaped out of the hole, a little too quickly.

In the final sentence the narrator "throws" his grandmother's medicine pouch into the grave. Though some readers find no humor in this passage, others discover the irony in Native Americans themselves dishonoring a burial. Blackfeet once used above-ground scaffolds to lay to rest their dead and began using burials only on the arrival of missionaries, and so the author underscores the absurdity of this "forced" western burial. Here the ancestral earth cannot accommodate such unwieldy losses. Critics are often divided on whether the narrator has healed the "winter in his blood": in throwing in the pouch does he turn from or reconnect with ancestors? This final passage invokes the Vanishing Indian and yet refuses it at every turn through irony and humor.

Literature as decolonization

A successful story re-creates the sacred order of the people in the universe, affirming what Laguna writer Leslie Silko calls a "communal truth" that renews the world. From these insights Native American critics have derived models for a Native literature that help nations recover from nothing less than genocide. Native American literature still raises consciousness: too often Native people, especially children, absorb narratives of defeated Indians and become as we say "internally colonized." But Native American literature can awaken us to inaccurate histories and damaging stereotypes, and thus embolden us not only to resist plunder of lands and resources, but also to revalue our own Native bodies and minds. Native American Studies promote literature as decolonization.

Native literary scholars remind us that service to the indigenous community may appear in many forms, from residing at home and revitalizing a language to living overseas and writing about Europeans. Indeed any rigid standard for Native American literary purpose is in the end self-defeating, for it dangerously narrows the space for Native imagining and invariably relies on the same litmus test of authenticity that misled anthropologists more than a century ago. In answering this question of authenticity again we need only look to Red Power and the emergence of Native American literary studies, where another essay continues to shape the field. In "Towards a National Indian Literature," Acoma poet Simon Ortiz begins with a story about his Uncle Steve, who used to participate in their fiesta days, in pueblo-wide ceremonies held on Catholic saints' days and that reenact the arrival of Spanish soldiers with Oñate in 1598. Uncle Steve was a fine dancer and would holler in Spanish the names of saints, and a man dressed as Oñate, his face painted in a hideous jeer, would curse the crowd, the children running in mock fear. Ortiz explains that the townspeople at Acoma are not seeking to perform the Catholic sacrament or even to imitate the ways of Spaniards. Instead they have taken a catastrophic event from their Acoma history—the vicious invasion of Spanish soldiers—and absorbed it "in the people's own terms" within Acoma consciousness, thereby defusing its ability to control, that is, to colonize them:

> And this, of course, is what happens in literature, to bring about meaning and meaningfulness. This perception and meaningfulness has to happen; otherwise the hard experience of the Euroamerican colonization of the lands and people of the Western hemisphere would be driven into the dark recesses of the indigenous mind and psyche. And this kind of repression is always a poison and detriment to creative growth and expression.

In his essay Ortiz replies to the anthropologist, who for a century searched for those Indians who were still "uncorrupted" by European arrival and, in the process, dismissed as "inauthentic" those other indigenous communities that did not satisfy the standard. Those who spoke English or Spanish or French or who performed an adulterated fragment of liturgy were among these. Ortiz, however, also offers his essay to other Native Americans who have internalized a component of colonialism that upholds this false standard still today. While some scholars may contend that Acoma is now a mixed or "hybrid" culture that blends both European and Acoma values and practices, Ortiz sees it differently. For him and many other Native critics it comes down to adaptation—and resistance. For this reason "new" knowledge may enter a community to be incorporated within an indigenous worldview. In fact Ortiz explains that this adaptive process is not simply artistic but indeed political. Native Americans consciously shape their bodies of knowledge with new practices, values, and even languages to resist domination and nurture indigenous nations: "This is the crucial item that has to be understood, that it is entirely possible for a people to retain and maintain their lives through the use of any language. There is no question of authenticity here; rather it is the way Indian people have creatively responded to forced colonization. And this response has been one of resistance; there is no clearer word for it than resistance."

In today's Native American literature characters return home, but may also leave for cities sometimes across the globe, where they learn to speak foreign languages and might plan to stay. It may be that to embrace this diversity in the literature will not threaten but in fact serve the cultural security of indigenous worlds. Perhaps owing to this travel Native literature today bears an international readership, and its quality and visibility have placed Native American literary scholars at the vanguard of Native American Studies. In his 1983 essay, Ortiz explains this expanding cycle of search through his father's song: "[T]he song was the road from outside of himself to the inside . . . and from inside of himself to outside."

Chapter 6
The Native novel

A Cherokee fugitive fantasizes about a bloody rampage against land thieves. A Creek suffragette dreams of becoming a white Christian woman. These two narratives form the first Native American novels, and they stand at the extreme reaches of resistance and assimilation to North American society. The first novel by a Native American—Cherokee newspaperman John Rollin Ridge's *Life and Adventures of Joaquin Murieta, the Celebrated California Bandit* (1854)—remains the goriest tale of armed reprisal for the theft of indigenous land, and the first novel by a Native woman—Creek writer Sophia Alice Callahan's *Wynema, a Child of the Forest* (1891)—remains the unparalleled story of Native American cultural shame and wholesale conversion to white Christian America. Since the publication of these first two novels, Native writers have used the form to test various responses to North American colonialism, from violent resistance to passive acceptance. The Native American novelist seeks to mediate, often subversively, between the "novel of resistance" and the "novel of assimilation."

By 1836 the Cherokee Nation had been invaded and terrorized by Georgians, and some Cherokees felt its removal was imminent. John Rollin Ridge's father, John Ridge, and a minority of Cherokee citizens signed a treaty to trade ancestral homelands for land west of Arkansas. For selling land without consent of the nation—by

Cherokee law a capital offense—a band of men impaled John Ridge in front of his son. John Rollin Ridge vowed revenge and eventually killed a man he suspected to be one of his father's assassins. Fleeing to the California gold fields, he endured his nation's removal and his own banishment by imagining himself the California bandit Joaquin Murieta, the Hispanic folk hero who on being routed from his home robs the wealthy to support the weak throughout the land. As a fugitive with fairer skin, a beard, and a western education, Ridge could have assimilated into the North American mainstream as a journalist in California. Instead he wrote behind his Indian name of Yellow Bird both to disguise his identity and, ironically, to declare his Indianness. Murieta briefly reveals his true self: "He dashed along that fearful trail as he had been mounted upon a spirit-steed, shouting as he passed: 'I am Joaquin! kill me if you can!'" Here only for a moment, the Cherokee rides a "spirit-steed" with "his long black hair streaming behind him." As author of the first indigenous novel of resistance, Yellow Bird was indeed far ahead of his time.

A Creek woman, Alice Callahan shares with John Rollin Ridge a similar history of dispossession and removal from the Southeast to Indian Territory, but in *Wynema* she does not question federal plans to displace nations and erase culture in order to "civilize" Native Americans. In this novel the white Methodist teacher Genevieve Weir, working in the Creek Nation, finds in the Creek woman Wynema all the promise of a wealthy Southern lady. Genevieve largely remains at the center of this sentimental novel of women's rights, and Wynema herself dreams of fulfilling Genevieve's suffragette visions of virtue: "we are waiting for our more civilized white sisters to gain their liberty, and thus set us an example which we shall not be slow to follow." Unlike Ridge, Callahan seems to accept the injustices of Indian removal and the ongoing destruction of culture as the unavoidable, even fortunate consequences of the advancement of North American industry and society west into indigenous lands. Her hope is that Native people may cast off their outmoded cultural ways to achieve full citizenship in settler nations in this first Native American novel of assimilation.

Few Native novels submit so willingly. Instead, Native American novelists, while rupturing colonial narratives, on the one hand, have cultivated indigenous social consciousness, on the other. To do so through the generations the Native novel of resistance has had to accommodate a spectrum of responses that ramify the most apparent forms of colonial challenge. Though resistance may include alternative narratives of tribal homecomings and cultural revivals, the portrayal of Native American resistance has shifted in the contemporary Native novel: no longer must Native Americans reject all western culture and return home to their reserves to fight their colonization. Instead, those activities viewed as assimilation in the early twentieth century—moving to the city, attending college, wearing a suit, traveling to Europe—now may appear as resistance to dominant assumptions that Indians cannot do such things.

Modern problems

Historians recognize the turn of the twentieth century as marking the depth of Native American populations and cultural vitality in North America. After centuries of state-sponsored destruction of indigenous cultures and economies, most indigenous nations and their governments had been reduced to utter dependence on colonial governments and their social planners, who saw the originary ways of Native people as impossible to maintain and even as the cause of their malaise. By the early twentieth century white and Native American leaders committed to "Indian uplift" through organizations such as the Society of American Indians (SAI) sought to prepare Native people for citizenship by eradicating the last of their traditional cultures. Native American writers no doubt felt the blows of this desperate era and some likely succumbed to the prevailing view that the only hope for Native survival was to forego ancestral ways and to assimilate into

North American society. Such novelists offered plots that place white culture at the center, which marginalized Native Americans aspire to reach.

Some novels by Cherokee writer John Milton Oskison perhaps best exemplify the Native American novel of assimilation. Educated at Stanford and Harvard, editor and feature writer of *Collier's Magazine*, and active member of the SAI, Oskison wrote such novels as *Wild Harvest* (1925) and *Black Jack Davy* (1926). Set in Indian Territory before Oklahoma statehood, these novels treat the arrival of white settlers as pivotal events wherein to negotiate cultural changes. Perhaps most developed of his novels is *Brothers Three* (1935). The novel uses the struggle of three brothers to keep the family farm as an emblem of the cultural challenges facing Native people, in which the autobiographical third son returns from New York as a writer and investor to help his family. Saving the farm has shaped many plots in the American novel, and here the central Native American characters promote values of hard work and thrift in hard times. To recognize indigenous cultural issues Oskison allows traditional Native characters to make occasional entrances as minor players in the drama.

While many have agreed that Oskison argued for Native American assimilation, a posthumously published 1930s novel, *The Singing Bird*, might suggest an unknown resistance in the author. The novel portrays life in the 1820s at the Dwight Mission School to the Western Cherokees, but it takes a dramatic turn with the appearance of a fictionalized Sequoyah, the inventor of the Cherokee written language. The mission school narrative frame recedes to foreground a subplot surrounding Sequoyah's search for the Lost Cherokee in Mexico. Oskison imagines Sequoyah seeking in that fabled land the "sacred symbols" recording ancient Cherokee history. Here Oskison's missionary Dan Wear considers Sequoyah's scholarly quest: "...after their loss there was unrest and spiritual discontent amongst the people....[H]e hopes to

restore the faith of the Cherokees in their old god." Though Oskison still places white missionaries at the novel's center, Native Americans here seek and believe in their own symbols, literature, "old god," and sovereign nation. During this time Choctaw writer Todd Downing also looked to Mexico in several crime novels, including *The Cat Screams* (1934).

In 1928 the Department of the Interior received the Meriam Report, a federally mandated study of social and economic conditions among Native Americans. It revealed the disastrous consequences of allotment and federal bureaucracy on reservations. In response the Franklin D. Roosevelt administration's Commissioner of Indian Affairs John Collier introduced the Wheeler-Howard Indian Reorganization Act (IRA) of 1934, known as the Indian New Deal, to restore Native self-government. As a result, modernity made its way to indigenous communities. While assimilationist novels primarily presented realist plots and characters, other Native American writers employed modernist techniques to question the necessity or even the possibility of Native people entering the mainstream.

The modern Native American novel began around this time with the publication of Osage writer John Joseph Mathews's *Sundown* (1934) and Salish writer D'Arcy McNickle's *Surrounded* (1936). In *Sundown* Chal Windsor leaves his Osage reservation to attend university, then becomes an aviator and travels the globe in World War I. Years later he returns home, only to find his community unbearably small. His mixed Osage father advises assimilation into North American society, his Osage mother a return to Osage customs. Unable to reconcile his yearning for discovery abroad with the call to traditional life at home, Chal buckles under depression and alcoholism. Mathews variously inflects Chal's story with either realist or modernist conventions at key moments. Those spent with his mother or gazing at Osage lands Matthews presents with realistic clarity. When Chal attends college, rushes a fraternity, or encounters the destructive force of alcohol, modernist fragmentation gains full expression. In longing for but foregoing life beyond the nation, Mathews does not resign to assimilation so much as he imagines the possibility of a cosmopolitan, even transnational Native American future.

In *The Surrounded*, after wandering around Oregon playing the fiddle, Archilde Leon returns home to his Flathead Reservation. Archilde's white father asks him finally to submit to mainstream society, while his Flathead mother, living in a dirt-roofed log cabin away from her husband, invites Archilde to embrace his people's originary culture. With this work McNickle set the prototype of the Native American novel most recognized by contemporary audiences, complete with its treatment of colonialism and the power of oral traditions to resist it. Though McNickle's novels develop complex protagonists to ask difficult questions about ancestral knowledge, cultural identity, and colonial change, he ultimately suggests that Native Americans will either exist in flux between the conflicting demands of two cultures or simply self-destruct. When Archilde visits his mother's family and observes a traditional dance, he feels somehow embarrassed and out of place: "They were not real people." During a hunting trip to the mountains he witnesses his mother murder a white game warden, leaving him further disoriented and unmoored. He has thrown off his western culture but can find no comfort or protection on his indigenous road of resistance that leads only deeper into the mountains.

For decades McNickle worked on his most complex novel, *Wind from an Enemy Sky*, published posthumously in 1978, about two elder Native brothers, one a revered chief and the other an assimilated farmer, who have grown apart over the years but are now brought together by a terrible event. The government has dammed the river that has sustained the Little Elk people for generations; in reprisal, a young member of the camp has killed a worker at the dam. Later an anthropologist claims to have located in a museum the Little Elk people's invaluable beaver medicine,

Native American Literature

90

the power of which promises to save the people. The anthropologist discovers, however, that the bundle had been left to rot in the museum's basement and so offers the Little Elks a Peruvian artifact instead. Such absurdly sad miscommunications between the Native Americans and the white settlers continue a chain of tragic events in *Wind from an Enemy Sky*, through which McNickle again shares his conclusions that western and indigenous worldviews are ultimately incommensurable.

One might also credit McNickle with developing the subgenre of the Native American historical novel that asserts a forgotten history to serve resistance. Reared on the early hope that John Collier would return national autonomy to Native people under the IRA, McNickle spent the years 1936 to 1952 working for the Bureau of Indian Affairs (BIA). On seeing the federal government begin to terminate its legal relationship with indigenous nations with the 1953 House Concurrent Resolution 108, McNickle resigned. His sense of betrayal and pessimism marks the above novels, and perhaps explains his wish to write historical fiction. A year later, McNickle published *Runner in the Sun*, a young adult novel. The author imagines pre-contact times in the cliff-dwelling Southwest, when indigenous people faced a different threat. The novel's elders scold the young hero, Salt, for seeking scientific explanations for their worsening draught and for suggesting their own beliefs on the subject might be superstitious. The banished Holy One sends Salt on a journey to discover a solution to the crisis in Mesoamerica, where Salt finds a new strain of corn and a new religious symbol to ensure their survival. In this final novel, the author offers here a positive vision of crisis, change, and renewal to indigenous communities.

While one could argue that such work of historical fiction is escapist, here McNickle leads Native youths to an earlier time when western invasions were not the source of their crisis. Instead readers see how an earlier indigenous community challenges those who abuse sacred knowledge through fear-mongering and intimidation, and how Native Americans use their scientific minds to identify and solve problems, seeking answers through hemispheric collaboration. Such historical fiction gained Native audiences, and perhaps for the same reasons then as today. Seeking a similar pre-contact history, Sioux anthropologist Ella Deloria's *Waterlily*, drafted in 1944 and published posthumously in 1988, returns to nineteenth-century Sioux life for a richly detailed account of camps, kinship, and religious and social customs.

By the 1980s Native American writers shared such returns with a broad audience. In James Welch's *Fools Crow* (1986), Blackfeet encounter not only encroaching soldiers and disease, but also generational differences and changing gender relations. Chickasaw writer Linda Hogan's *Mean Spirit* (1990) confronts corruption during the Osage oil boom. In later novels, Native American women writers utilize innovative themes of haunting and possession to integrate the present with visions of the past. LeAnne Howe's *Shell Shaker* (2001) imagines present-day sisters of the Billy family are drawn to the Choctaw Nation of the middle eighteenth century to witness the loving and gruesome clan sacrifice of Shakbatina, a woman leader who gives her life to restore peace. Sioux writer Susan Power's *Grass Dancer* (1995) haunts plains powwows with love potions and entrancing ghosts.

As early as 1927, with the publication of Mourning Dove's *Cogewea, the Half-Blood*, Native American authors harnessed the novel to engage problems of maintaining indigenous identities in the face of European colonization. Mourning Dove, a Salish, worked as a migrant laborer and wrote *Cogewea* in her tent at night. An Indian enthusiast named Lucullus McWhorter edited her manuscript, and eventually helped her publish the novel with his embellishments and in a very different form. McWhorter probably had much to do with changing Mourning Dove's work into a popular western romance, complete with villains and woeful pleas of half-breeds in distress, with epigraphs to each chapter taken from Longfellow's "Hiawatha," among other works. The novel opens on a Montana cattle ranch on the Flathead reservation where the cowboys are Indians of mixed ancestry. The young woman Cogewea lives with her Native family—her European father has left for the Alaska gold fields—and must decide among white and Native American suitors: the dastardly easterner Densmore or the silent hero, "breed" James LaGrinder. While this novel bears all the inconsistencies of an invasive editor at odds with its author, *Cogewea* displays the actual challenges facing mixed-race Native Americans at times barred from either culture when, for instance, Cogewea enters a horse race dressed as a white woman and wins. On discovery she loses her prize, the judge calling her a "squaw." And on entering a race for Native girls, she is told it is a race for Indians, not "breeds."

Red power novel

The Native American movements of the 1960s and 1970s provoked a new awareness of Native lives and possibilities. Settler governments soon shared this new consciousness. In the United States this drove passage of the 1975 Self-Determination Act to advance tribal self-governance, and in 1978 the Indian Child Welfare Act and the Religious Freedom Act to protect Native American families and customs. Such Red Power plans for the recovery of Native identity awakened the Native American novel. While McNickle and Mourning Dove treated mixed ancestry as evidence of cultural erosion, new writers saw indigenous identity, even mixed ancestry, as a solution to their colonial situation. Native writers adapted the novel to express the experience of political awakening on reconnection with indigenous land, community, and oral literature. Whereas the American novel tends to celebrate leaving home to develop one's character, the Red Power novel often relies on the opposite movement. Here Native Americans have already left home, and their stories begin on the cultural regeneration that marks their return. Still written today, such novels often actively enlist the alternative narrative practices of oral literature to reinterpret damaging colonized conclusions to recover indigenous identity, tribal experience, and cultural knowledge.

The title of N. Scott Momaday's first novel, *House Made of Dawn* (1968), refers to a Navajo healing ceremony to reintegrate community members as dwellers in the land. Momaday's protagonist Abel, home from World War II and estranged from his land, cannot recover his sense of place until he reimagines his own body belonging to home. In novels such as James Welch's *Winter in the Blood* (1974), authors broaden their interests from the individual to the community, using characters' vexed relationships to their environments as vehicles to discuss historical identifications with land. There a young Blackfeet man recovers an oral history about the ethical decisions of his ancestors, when he regains his masculinity and cultural identity. In Leslie Silko's *Ceremony* (1977), the Red Power novel engages political struggles to protect indigenous lands, as the protagonist Tayo recovers from a war that has damaged his ability to understand himself as a spiritual visionary.

By the 1980s some Native American novels began to question the pan-tribalism of the 1970s that sought to express a general Native cause at the expense of a distinct indigenous national experience. That redirection to community is explored in Okanagan author Jeannette Armstrong's *Slash* (1985). In Spokane and Coeur d'Alene writer Sherman Alexie's *Reservation Blues* (1995) three Spokane men start a blues band they call Coyote Springs and attempt to land a New York City record contract, but they fail. When asked about his community, Thomas Builds-the-Fire, the community's unofficial and unappreciated storyteller, remembers the layers of poverty they have all suffered: "Thomas thought about all the dreams that were murdered here, and the bones buried quickly just inches below the surface, all waiting to break through the foundations of those government houses built by the Department of Housing and Urban Development." The visceral suggestion of bone piercing skin introduces readers to the colonial wounds Spokane people continue to feel "just inches below the surface," for their dispossession is rather recent in the U.S. history of conquering Indians. The federal government hides these murders beneath cheap HUD concrete. From the novel's beginning, Thomas understands the source of Native American poverty, but he wonders how his people can even begin to dig through such layers, to dress the wounds, to lay the bones to rest.

While Alexie is firmly rooted in his Native community, many consider that Anishinaabe author Louise Erdrich perfects the art of writing about one's nation. In more than a dozen novels she approaches a single community from multiple viewpoints and historical periods. In her best-loved novel *Tracks* (1989), Erdrich asks readers to confront the devastating consequences of the Allotment Act, not only for Native American landholdings, but also for the social harmony of the community. Onondaga writer Eric Gansworth's *Smoke Dancing* (2004) shows the power of originary song and dance to weave Native people into communities.

Both pan-tribalism and national specificity found their way to the city, where they led to tension but also strength. Navajo writer Irvin Morris's *From the Glittering World* (2000) engages a restless movement away from and back to Navajo homelands. Morris's narrator leaves the safety of reservation territories to gain new perspectives of "my mother, the earth," and of the powers that threaten both his people and their land. At rock bottom in Gallup, he considers the source of his depression, addiction, and homelessness, and he finds fear at the heart of his reluctance to go home: "I am afraid to face my own life. I am Indian. I am minority. I am dark and I am powerless." Significantly, the narrator suggests that his experiences of the world beyond his nation have led him to "know too much," a condition that fuels his despair. In departures to the city the narrator discovers his life, best available to him at a safe distance from home, where "the sirens welcome me," but where he may also read "the tribal newspaper." Throughout *From the Glittering World*, the narrator learns to live with an ironic tension between reservation and city, between lived experience and read experience, where Native American life often makes more sense when seen from a distance.

In Pomo writer Greg Sarris's *Grand Avenue* (1994), Native people contend with life in a poor mixed black, Indian, Mexican, and white neighborhood on Grand Avenue in Santa Rosa, California. Native Americans here live in renovated army barracks where space is crowded but social relationships are strong. Like the Red Power writing of the 1960s and 1970s Sarris engages the Pomo past without denying the urban Native present in which oppressive conditions impede historical and personal knowledge. One day Nellie, a medicine woman, finds a curious girl in her garden. Nellie names various plants for the girl and notices "something old-time about this girl, maybe just the way she identified herself, telling her family line." The relationship that grows from this encounter links generations of Pomo people now living in the city. As the old and young women weave baskets together, they untangle and re-braid the old stories, and in the process come to understand their colonial pain. In the city kinship obligations endure and keep youths learning from elders to maintain an urban traditionalism.

Because the Native American urban novel grows from a desire for cultural and social exchange in cosmopolitan spaces, it has become a vehicle for Native writers who seek to address the lives of Native American women or of gay and lesbian Natives. Paula Gunn Allen's *Woman Who Owned the Shadows* (1983) imagines lesbian life in San Francisco, while Coeur d'Alene author Janet Campbell Hale's *Jailing of Cecelia Capture* (1985) has a protagonist gain a Berkeley law degree and discloses the legal control of low-income women. In Native women's novels such as Betty Louise Bell's *Faces in the Moon* (1994) or Louise Erdrich's *Love Medicine* (1984), Native American women are not always anchored to the earth by readily available female ways of knowing;

rather, they might find themselves in cities far from home and dominated by men. In such cases, as depicted in *Cecelia Capture*, Native women remember their social training or undergo a process of self-discovery, in which they disclose the reality of their gendered lives and find freedom. In jail for a DUI, Cecelia recounts how the past thirty years of her life have led her to her present bouts with alcohol and thoughts of suicide. Cecelia shares her cell with Velma, who notices Cecelia's wedding band and declares: "The only difference between a married woman and a whore ... is that they fuck just one dude and get paid a lot less." Here Velma introduces a central political claim in the novel: in this sexist world, autonomy for women in one area of life often comes in exchange for submission to men in another. Though demonized for selling sex, Velma justifies her work with an ethic that does not endanger lives or submit to men in marriage. In this novel a woman's crime is often just refusing to assimilate into North American masculinist culture.

While homosexual longing appears in Morris's *From the Glittering World* and Sarris's *Watermelon Nights* (1998), it receives full treatment in Craig Womack's *Drowning in Fire* (2001), in which historical fiction concerning the pre-statehood Creek Nation informs a modern coming-out narrative. In an innovative invocation of oral literature, the protagonist Josh realizes the awesome creative potential of indigenous story. Like the ancient earth diver, Josh has submerged to the depths of homosexual possibility but fears to emerge, for "what would I first utter?" He also imagines himself "flying" through the Native national past, but he realizes that he also must discover the courage to land. Finally his Aunt Lucille shows Josh how to search Creek history for language that will communicate his experiences.

Native American innovation

Leslie Silko's *Almanac of the Dead* (1991) draws its force from Native American women in cities. The novel overturns romantic assumptions of Native women as caregivers with an opening scene of elder sisters Leche and Zeta cooking up drugs in their kitchen: "The old woman stands at the stove stirring the simmering brown liquid with great concentration.... She glances up through the rising veil of steam at the young blond woman pouring pills from brown plastic prescription vials." Yet in its hemispheric scope combining historical events with indigenous prophecy, *Almanac of the Dead* is also a Native American novel of supreme innovation. In Linda Hogan's *Power* (1999), women are also at the center of a cataclysmic storm that threatens to destroy and reform human and animal relationships. Using experimental prose, the author presents a distressing ethical debate on Native sovereignty versus animal rights.

Indeed, from its inception and by necessity the Native American novel has been experimental, attracting and modifying subgenres to seek Native cultural survival and development. In the phalanx of political movements during the past century, Native writers have made the novel their place of both formal and social innovation. In formal terms Native American authors experiment with plot formulae, self-conscious narration, or novelistic expectations; in cultural terms they place Native people in unexpected conversations that discover new possibilities for indigenous lives. Authors such as Gerald Vizenor made the novel a place to imagine the relationship of intellectual health to Native American cultural health, what he calls "survivance." In his sexually violent and controversial fantasy novel of apocalyptic pilgrimage, *Bearheart* (1978), Vizenor offers a message on dogmatic thinking. Belladonna Darwin-Winter Catcher is simplistic about her indigenousness. So when she encounters "the hunter," he executes her with a poison cookie, declaring that she "is a terminal believer and a victim of her own narcissism." These Native American novels are difficult to place in part because they refuse to surrender explicit meanings. In *Monkey Beach* (2000), Haisla and Heiltsuk author Eden Robinson loses us in the island communities of her homeland in British Columbia, where a

troubled young woman searches for her missing fisherman brother. The land's misty silence and the novel's dreamy language lull readers into imagining orcas and sasquatch and to accept their many mysteries.

As calls for greater autonomy from settler governments are increasingly answered, Native American authors will continue to expand the artistic and cultural reach of the Native novel. James Welch imagines the ethical consequences of Native people achieving advanced degrees and entering politics in *The Indian Lawyer* (1990), only further to test Native American travel narratives in *The Heartsong of Charging Elk* (2000). Here Sioux warrior Charging Elk sails to France to perform in a Wild West show, where he falls ill, remains behind, and decides to stay to form a new family. Cherokee writer Thomas King's *Truth and Bright Water* (1999) offers two eponymous towns, one Native and the other white, that straddle the U.S.-Canada border in an internationally boundary-busting novel. Mesquakie writer Ray Young Bear's *Remnants of the First Earth* (1996) explores the power of including poetic imagery in prose, where fantasy cannot be distinguished from reality, and whole passages appear in Mesquakie untranslated.

The Native American novel has become increasingly aware of itself as an art with real-world consequences for Native lives. David Treuer's *Hiawatha* (1999) seizes the power of uncompromising plot devices and traumatized language. Set in post-relocation Minneapolis, this novel is a dirge for assimilation, offering resistance in language itself, or in acts of violence. Such violence, no matter how literary or its colonial causes, remains an unsettling trend in some Native American novels. In James Welch's *Death of Jim Loney* (1979) Loney sees no possibility of resistance and kills himself; and in Sherman Alexie's *Indian Killer* (1996) a Native serial killer is said to stalk the city streets taking white men's scalps. Ojibwe writer Richard Wagamese invites reflection on the Native American novel and its creation and purposes not with dead-end force but with the care of family, elders, and community in his *Keeper 'n Me* (1994). At three years Garnet Raven was taken from his Ojibwe family by the state and given to a white family. When he is twenty and in prison, his birth family discovers him and calls him home. It is an unassuming story of family forgiveness, cultural revival, and spiritual cleansing. Thomas King teaches with similar self-mocking humor. In *Green Grass, Running Water* (1994), white tourists visit the community's Dead Dog Café to see "real" Indians and to taste what they believe to be traditional dog meat hamburgers. Throughout, the narrator even reprimands the oral traditional Coyote figure (and presumably the rest of us) to "pay attention" and "forget about being helpful"; just "sit down and listen."

In writing the first Native American novel, John Rollin Ridge likely sought social refuge and intellectual health as much as artistic discovery or celebrity. With returns to tradition, but also innovation and travel, the Native novel continues to serve colonial resistance. Perhaps in the spirit of Yellow Bird, today's Native American writers have awakened, rekindled their fires, and breathed into the novel an indigenous voice for national autonomy, cultural persistence, and social pluralism.

Chapter 7
Indigenous futurity

Cherokees traditionally planted "white eagle corn." On each differently colored kernel there appears a white shape resembling an eagle in flight. In 1838 they carried these seeds west during the removal, and in 2014 the Cherokee Nation distributed the kernels from its seed bank to citizens to help them revive their ancient diet. The Cherokee Nation decided to restore its time-honored corn crop not because it came from the pre-contact past but, rather, because it may help to secure its indigenous future.

Such indigenous revivals might be viewed as expressions of "futurity," operating in resistance to those assumptions that consign Native American peoples and lifeways to the past. From their first arrivals in the Western Hemisphere, explorers envisioned that new land and its people as outside of history. For America did not exist in the Christian Bible and was thus beyond the reach of time itself. Columbus for instance informed Ferdinand and Isabella that he had discovered Eden. Inheriting this perspective, settlers often viewed their landing in the New World as a preordained return to a prelapsarian moment. Europeans bound for the future thus were destined to supplant Indians trapped in the past. Yet even though Native people did not see themselves as anachronisms programmed for extinction, they still shared no divine destiny to expand with American "progress." Instead they planned a sustainable future, a future that was disrupted by conquest. On the reemergence of Native American literature in the 1970s, N. Scott Momaday finally revived this futurity. He beckoned Native people to imagine a new life, a life closer to the land and to the stories. In so doing they would embrace their indigenous futurity.

In the 1950s the United States increasingly pressured Native Americans to leave their communities for urban centers. But by the early 1960s, with the emergence of the National Indian Youth Council, Native communities sought futures on their own terms by reaffirming what Ponca intellectual Clyde Warrior called their "worthiness." This worth was proclaimed in 1969 with the publication of Momaday's mixed genre work, *The Way to Rainy Mountain*. In this work the author imagines a "way" home for Native people wherein Kiowas return to their oral histories and adapt ethnography to reconnect with ancestors and plan a future. Progress may lead Native Americans off to cities, but it occurs just as much at home among members of the community, revitalizing ceremony or recording story. With the passing of the Indian Gaming Regulatory Act in 1988 and the Native American Graves

9. The Apache leader Geronimo was released briefly from prison to pose for this photograph in 1904. Perhaps the photographer wished to juxtapose what he considered symbols of America's past and future.

Protection and Repatriation Act in 1990, federal legislation promoted Native economies and repatriated ceremonial objects and burial remains to homelands. In viewing this pattern of return and revitalization in Native nations, one discerns an alternative model of advancement: progress as directing material and creative resources not toward growth but toward persistence. Here ceremony, economy, and literature offer life within valued community patterns for present and future generations. It is progress as sustainability.

Since buttressing the sovereign status of indigenous nations in the 1970s, settler governments have seen Native communities attract the dollars of tourism, gaming, or industry, for instance. The Pequots now operate the most profitable casino in the world, and the Cherokee Nation is one of the largest employers in Oklahoma. Native American communities often direct those new profits to infrastructure: housing programs, nutrition and fitness campaigns, scholarships, indigenous language revitalization, national museums, even the purchase of ancestral lands.

It is the same new song

The most voluminous of all Native American literature remains the song. Indigenous songs vary widely in their content and purposes from nation to nation, but most all of them recognize the power of language to address and even alter the universe. Enchanted words can divert a storm, bring a harvest or a child, heal an illness, repel an enemy, or win a lover. Native American poets invoke this ancient power of song, at times even offering a poem as a "song." For these reasons indigenous oral literatures readily adapt poetry, and poetry enjoys widespread popular appeal in Native communities. Native American youth enter "poetry slams," perhaps as a continuation of long-standing patterns of communal performance. As a young writer Sherman Alexie won three poetry slam championships, and Santa Fe Indian School's

Slam Poets yearly compete in the Brave New Voices International Youth Festival in Washington, DC. Native American poetry today promises a populist futurity.

Nineteenth-century Native poets such as Jane Johnston Schoolcraft and John Rollin Ridge, as well as early-twentieth-century poets such as E. Pauline Johnson, Alexander Posey, Zitkala-Ša, and Iroquois Frank James Prewett, have long turned classical poetic forms toward indigenous content. Audiences especially celebrated Johnson, a Mohawk woman from the Lake Ontario area, for her oral poetic performances; today readers equally value her insightful short stories. Only recently have scholars amassed the body of nineteenth-century Native American poetry from newspapers and archives. By the late twentieth century a number of Native poets received extensive formal training: N. Scott Momaday studied with Yvor Winters at Stanford, and James Welch and Roberta Hill worked with Richard Hugo at the University of Montana. Such poets continued to adapt western poetic forms to express indigenous realities, at times even using rhyme and lyric, sonnets and sestinas. Since the 1970s most Native American poets have worked in free verse, though often altering form and mixing genre. Whatever the form, contemporary Native poets look to oral literature and its long-held understanding of language as a source of change. Such poetry not only frees Native American voices, but also confirms a spiritual awareness of ancestral land and community.

Simon Ortiz offers poems as gifts to embolden not only Native, but also any people to love and defend the land. While he also writes essays and short stories, the poetic form might enable for him a kind of alchemy unavailable in other genres, a rarified space in which to compress image and sound, to juxtapose historical moments or communal memories. In "A Story of How a Wall Stands," Ortiz narrates a conversation with his father about the construction of an ancient stone wall that supports a cemetery in his ancestral town. The son tells the father it appears ready to crumble but while repairing the wall the father replies: "'That's just the part you see, / the stones which seem to be / just packed in on the outside'…. 'Underneath what looks like loose stone, / there is stone woven together.'" Perhaps the son reveals his youth and impatience with the craft of ancestors, but the father asks the son to imagine more than the eye can see, to honor the careful design of a wall meant to preserve and connect the generations. The lines break with the breath of work, of lifting and fitting stone. With gritty sound and warm texture the father also describes the ties of indigenous story: "He tells me those things, / the story of them worked / with his fingers, in the palm / of his hands, working the stone / and the mud until they become / the wall that stands a long, long time." Here indigenous narrative requires patient labor across the generations as imbricated in stones. For Ortiz, stories carefully mended together will be the design to cement the people. In such "centering" poems Ortiz and other Native American poets claim their futurity.

In "Empty Kettle," Creek poet Louis Little Coon Oliver declares sustainable values—"I do not waste what is wild / I only take what my cup / can hold"—and celebrates the call to hunt when "the black kettle gapes / empty." He prepares with a chant: "I chant the deer chant:/"He-hebah-Ah-kay-kee-no!" then on killing the deer seeks balance in the taking: "I open the way for the blood to pour / back to Mother Earth / the debt I owe." Having fed his children, he sings: "My soul rises—rapturous / and I sing a different song, / I sing, / I sing." Like "A Story of How a Wall Stands," "Empty Kettle" proclaims the values that sustain people across generations, and affirms human reciprocal ties to land, here in the hunter's returning the deer's blood to the earth. Such poems validate men's nurturing, to weave stone or hunt meat for the generations. Invoking chant and song such poems enlist the revitalizing potential of language.

Equally often, however, Native American poets call on the genre to confront injustice. James Welch's "The Man from Washington" recalls the arrival of a federal official to a nineteenth-century reservation, with Native people recently "Packed away in our crude beginnings / in some far corner of a flat world." With bitter irony the narrator understands the mainstream perception of his people as crowded into a reservation, remote from European ways, primitives with irrational minds who still believe in a "flat world." Or if from this pre-contact world, they should not even exist. Yet the official is also obscure, a "slouching dwarf with rainwater eyes," a broken emissary crying improbable tears. Such a man from Washington cannot be trusted: "He promised / that life would go on as usual / that treaties would be signed, and everyone— / man, woman, and child—would be inoculated / against a world in which we had no part, / a world of money, promise, and disease." The bison eradicated, their lands stolen, all know that life cannot possibly "go on as usual," and even "inoculation" against European diseases will not protect them from colonial modernity and their "diseased" economy.

Other Native American poets ask us to return to crucial historical moments in the conquest of Native peoples. In *From Sand Creek* (1981), Simon Ortiz revisits the Sand Creek Massacre when in 1864 "the fighting parson" John Chivington slaughtered Southern Cheyennes camping in southern Colorado. The poet does not shame mainstream readers for inheriting the benefits of the atrocity. Instead Ortiz invites meditation on the land and its own suffering, the minds of white settlers, the hopes of Native Americans. However, he will not downplay the evil of American voters and their leaders, including Chivington's men, who "deemed / themselves blessed and pure / so that not even breath / became life— / life strangled / in their throats. Blood / gurgled and ran backwards / and swirled them into a whirl / of greed and callousness." The hunting, the cutting down and cutting out emerge as a dark song in which life-giving breath is now death— the very inversion of indigenous sacred song. Ultimately seeking to heal, Ortiz views other futures written on the land: "but, look now, / there are flowers / and new grass / and a spring wind / rising / from Sand Creek."

In "Indian Boarding School: The Runaways," Louise Erdrich gives voice to Native American children who endured residential and boarding schools. The adult children remain haunted by the brutality: "Home's the place we head for in our sleep." As children they flee to hop a train home, in which their very mode of escape paradoxically is also their abuse: "The rails, old lacerations that we love, / shoot parallel across the face and break / just under Turtle Mountains." Scars of trauma never fade, but they recur in nightmares: "The worn-down welts / of ancient punishments lead back and forth." Navajo poet Laura Tohe also revisits the boarding schools in *No Parole Today* (1999).

In her book-length return to personal, family, and indigenous national trauma, *A Map to the Next World* (2000), Creek poet Joy Harjo draws on multiple genres to find a path to healing. At the end of that path is a "next world" where enemies are vanquished and the body and spirit can thrive. Harjo's map is global: some poems describe a view from above the Southwest, others travel across the world. Whirlwinds and whorls recur, suggesting a climbing, spiraling quest for the next world's aperture. The project calls for a search that enlists all senses, especially touch, and declares bodily pleasure to heal memories of abuse: "In the dark I travel by instinct, / through the rubble of nightmares, / groaning of monsters toward the crack of light / along your body's horizon." While this search requires a communal self, Harjo also celebrates the portable power contained within the individual: "Your skin is the map."

Eric Gansworth returns to an impoverished reservation childhood. In poems such as "Dream House" the narrator, like the boarding school runaways, is haunted nightly by a dream of his childhood home that is anything but a "dream house." He peers through his bedroom window, "pane shrouded / in cloudy winter plastic / a cataract obscuring life / beyond the barrier / where we all dreamed awake / of some other existence / beyond the reservation." The plastic weatherproofs the window in a drafty, poorly heated house, but comes to stand for a better world flaunted forever out of reach. The "shrouded" "pane" of this window homophonically evokes the "pain" of viewing with poor vision another life. Though the narrator finally overcomes that transparent barrier, as an adult in a well-heated home he still has nightmares. One day years ago the "dream house" burned to the ground and the narrator wonders in his sleepless nights if he could "reform" his dreams "support by desperate / support," as he seeks to end the trauma by rebuilding that dream house of the mind.

In "No Pie," Ojibwe poet Mark Turcotte recalls a boy's trip with his white mother off the reservation to get a slice of pie. "And I remember my mother's pearl-white hands / twisting the lid from her secret Mason jar." Seated at the counter of a diner, the boy "knocked / together the dangling toes of my tattered sneakers." As the boy gazes at "the fat pies lined up neatly behind the glass," his mother asks for two pieces of pie, one apple, one pumpkin, but the waitress replies that they sell only whole pies. Unable to afford a whole pie they depart feeling the irrational shame of poverty. On the drive home he sat "staring at my small brown fists" and "turned / to watch the world speed by, both our mouths / filled with tears." Here Turcotte redeems the worn image of apple pie as a symbol of America, of pumpkin pie as an image of Thanksgiving, the Indian holiday. Like the obscured window in "Dream Home," the partitioned pies offer the inaccessible promise of a middle-class life. He cannot have only a piece of the pie in a system where the winner takes all. The boy learns this hard lesson about class and is silenced by the crisis, stalled as the "world speeds by," his mouth filled not with pie but tears.

Acting out

When in 1914 the photographer Edward Curtis traveled to Vancouver to produce a film on the island's indigenous people, he found that cast members were already well-trained actors. Local Kwakwaka 'wakws had been performing their own grand ceremonies, complete with stages and sets, costumes and masks, for centuries. Across Native North America such ritual performances, from Navajo beautyway ceremonies and Hopi kachina dances in the Southwest to sun dances and sacred arrow ceremonies on the Great Plains to Iroquois midwinter ceremonies in the East and green corn ceremonies in the South, enact the very oral literatures that explain the origins and confirm the values of Native American peoples. Such ancient performances re-create the universe. While Native songs can effect change, these are often included within Native ritual drama as it embodies an entire indigenous world. In its profound capacity to sustain Native Americans, centuries-old performance finds a close affinity with modern theater. Today's Native people may find a healthier venue for "acting out," not as Freud's defensive tantrum but to root themselves in land as a community and enact their future.

At the time of Curtis's production, Native Americans playwrights had little control over the mainstream stage. By the 1930s, however, Cherokee dramatist Lynn Riggs wrote twenty-one full-length plays, including *Green Grow the Lilacs* (1931), which Rogers and Hammerstein adapted to become *Oklahoma!* Riggs considered as most important his only play with entirely Native content, *The Cherokee Night* (1932). In this work the playwright displays a keen understanding of the conflicts facing Native Americans wishing to retain their cultures but fearing persecution and poverty. In one exchange, sisters Viney and Sarah debate acculturation; Viney has thoroughly westernized while Sarah remains closer to her indigenousness. Sarah attacks Viney: "You've turned your back on what you ought to a-been proud of." Viney fires back: "Being part-Indian? What would it get me? Do you think I want to be ignorant and hungry and crazy in my head half the time like a lot of 'em around here?" Clearly Riggs was aware of the psychological cost of being Native in a world that punishes it.

Not until the Native American movements of the 1970s did Native theater fully emerge. In 1972 Kiowa and Delaware playwright

Hanay Geiogamah founded the first long-standing Native American theater company, what came to be known as the Native American Theater Ensemble (NATE). In 1975 Muriel Miguel and other women created the Brooklyn-based Spiderwoman Theater, which became the longest running women's theater in the United States. Central to their company is their concept of "storyweaving," a process that melds nonhierarchical feminist narratives with indigenous oral literatures. Their name invokes Grandmother Spider, the deity who in Hopi oral literature taught Hopis to weave. In *Winnetou's Snake Oil Show from Wigwam City* (1988), Spiderwoman Theater plays with stereotypes and spiritual appropriations, then ends with serious statements on Native women's identity. Native American theater often focuses on indigenous oral narratives or contemporary social issues and readily infuses the stage with song and drum music, for instance, but, like other forms, it is often challenged to reshape the genre to meet the formal needs of Native narratives. Much of western literature relies on opposition; the novel, for example, must have characters and plot, and plot relies on conflict. Native American dramatists such as Drew Hayden Taylor, who is Ojibwe, argue that such conflict is often foreign to indigenous oral literatures.

During the 1980s several other Native theaters appeared, and for the first time theater about Native Americans was Native written, cast, and run. These theaters produced plays by Assiniboine and Sioux dramatist William Yellow Robe, Comanche playwright Terry Gomez, and LeAnne Howe, among many others. Geiogamah envisioned a Native American theater movement adapting the stage to indigenous models of performance, including ritual drama, song, and chant, but also addressing Native social issues. Navajo company members Geraldine Keams, Robert Shorty, and Timothy Clashin developed *Na Haaz Zaan*, an adaptation of Keams's grandmother's telling of the Navajo creation, which on an evening in 1972 they staged in Navajo with English translations on various set levels to dramatize the layered Navajo worlds. For their second performance the same evening NATE staged Geiogamah's

10. The Miguel sisters of Spiderwoman Theater pose in character for *Reverb-Ber-Ber-Rations* (1994), a performance about growing up Native American and building a spiritual community through the generations. Spiderwoman Theater is the longest running women's theater in the United States.

best known and most controversial play, *Body Indian*, in which several Native Americans in a messy Oklahoma City apartment spend allotment lease money on wine. Having lost his leg while inebriated on some railroad tracks, Bobby Lee limps into his uncle's apartment, a bag of wine bottles under one arm. The bottle passes while Bobby slurs a wish to enter rehab and his "relatives" ridicule his plans. After Bobby passes out, they nervously search him for his allotment money, removing his prosthesis to discover his hidden cash. In this troubling image Bobby's dismembered body evokes the railroad's role in westward expansion and the concurrent fracture of communal land relationships consequent to the Dawes Act. He is literally severed by the railroad, figuratively severed from his land. Bobby is inadequately compensated through the allotment money that he uses to seek wholeness by literally stuffing the cavity of his prosthesis with the dollars, and he fills his Indian body with the wine the allotment money buys.

The twenty-first-century Native American stage often defiantly refuses colonial borders, and indigenous playwrights in Canada, such as Daniel David Moses, Monique Mojica, and Tomson Highway, see their works performed throughout North America as they empower Native communities toward a sustaining and satisfying future. Cree dramatist Highway was born in 1951 in a tent on his father's trap line on an island in northern Manitoba. He spoke only Cree until entering a residential school and later living in foster homes. In college he studied to be a concert pianist before becoming a playwright. *Rez Sisters* (1986), the staging of seven reserve women who hope that bingo is their ticket to freedom, won best play in Toronto that season and toured Canada. That play's companion, *Dry Lips Oughta Move to Kapuskasing* (1989), revisits the imaginary Wasaychigan Hill Indian Reserve, this time focusing on seven men. Each embodies the different wounds to Native masculinity haunted by colonialism and Christianity, alcoholism and rape. Unlike many mainstream men's narrative, women oversee and intervene in this indigenous drama; the women even form a hockey team that threatens but also enlivens the men. At the core of both plays is the trickster figure found in oral literature. In *Dry Lips*, the Ojibwe trickster Nanabush is female and appears as various "Wasy" women in stage productions that include a hovering Nanabush and a honky-tonk jukebox.

A new indigenous experiment

D'Arcy McNickle's *Surrounded* (1936) ends tragically when Archilde Leon sees his mother murder a white game warden and, confused and afraid, flees into the wilderness. McNickle, in fact, began his novel with a different title; Native Americans were not "surrounded" but were "hungry generations." In *The Hungry Generations* Archilde actually finds happy resolution. After the murder he even travels to Paris where he experiences the expatriate literati and falls in love with a Frenchwoman. Like other Native American authors, McNickle had to negotiate with a

1930s white readership who harbored a view that Native people should not travel abroad, explore European art, and, above all, pursue romance with white women. In the years since *The Surrounded* appeared, however, Native American writers in all genres increasingly resist publishing venues still wishing to see the Vanishing Indian. Today they express an indigenous world in all its complexity, denying readers the colonial narratives and stereotypes that damage not only Native people but all of us. No longer will Native Americans be an "experiment" in civilization. Instead Native poets and playwrights, essayists and novelists initiate their own experiments with literary meanings and forms, plots and devices.

In *The Lesser Blessed* (1996), Dogrib writer Richard Van Camp places his indigenous protagonist far from ancestral lands in an impoverished all-white town in the Northwest Territories, Canada. Larry carries a dark secret but reveals little to us, aside from his hidden scars and fleeting memories of cousins, gasoline, and fire. His friend's little brother hides cigarette burns on his hands. Van Camp refuses to indulge the desire of some readers to dwell on Native dysfunction, and he even insists on a measure of privacy—or sovereignty—within the public genre of the novel. Larry lives in the comfort of his Dogrib culture when he is at home, but readers do not see Dogrib ceremony, custom, or practice. Instead, Van Camp credits young Natives with consciousness of cultural threats and class warfare that here begin in the white high school classroom:

> One day we were having this huge debate about whether it was environment or upbringing that creates a criminal. I looked around. Wasn't it fucking obvious? With the quiet bleeding labour of shellfish in our lockers. The sweet rotting flesh of our feet. The fluorescent lights making me weakdizzydemented. The crab cream two desks over. The gum under my desk. The spits on the floor. The silverfish. The crunch under my runners. The bleeding badge of the sun. The crunch under my runners. My father's teeth. The crunch

under my runners. Kevin Garner was selling drugs in the back row. Clarence Jarome was jamming his HB pencil into the primer of a 12-gauge slug. Everybody in the room, as their bodies cooled out, had their eyes fusing shut.

While the scene evokes other "blackboard jungles," one discerns a Native youth fully aware of the colonizing press of institutions. Ironically the students in their resignation answer the question for Mr. Harris. However here Larry displays a gift in language— surreal escape to sea, sound of snow underfoot—that promises his survival in this mean town.

Other Native American writers direct their work toward Van Camp's newer generation of readers, who seek narratives that appeal as much to the ear as to the eye. More and more Native illustrators are teaming up with Native American writers to imagine narratives that harness the richness of visual culture. In Tom Pomplun's *Native American Classics* (2013), ten indigenous illustrators give pictorial life to the central works of Native American literature, such as those by Charles Eastman, E. Pauline Johnson, Alexander Posey, and Zitkala-Ša. In *Trickster* (2010), nearly two dozen Native oral trickster stories from across North America find graphic illustration.

Often Native American writers proclaim their futurity by appropriating western genres or the treasured symbols of American progress. Sioux poet Tiffany Midge enlists frontier mythology for *Outlaws, Renegades, and Saints* (1996). Here Midge's parents are "fighting like cowboys and Indians" while she explicitly defies "tradition": "Forget your rules and tradition, / your social teas, religion and pearl / colored linens, I ain't like all the rest / of your sisters, 'cuz I'm a rodeo queen, / a cowgirl, a bulldogger. Whatever propriety I lack / is your problem, 'cuz I always knew that I'd go far!" Eric Gansworth's *Breathing the Monster Alive* (2006) faces his childhood dread of Bigfoot, the mythic primate of indigenous lore. The poet allows the mystery of this beast to consume him, plumbing the recesses of his imagination, its irrational fears and fascinations, where some settlers in Arkansas discovered "there was something / odd in the woods, down near the bottoms / where we'd built our first house." Gansworth fills his book with illustrations to bring visual culture to the poetry. In exploring the psychological depths of American popular culture, Gansworth inserts indigenous people within a contemporary world.

Other Native authors simply defy their genre. In *Up from These Hills* (2011), Leonard Lambert delivers a bluntly honest account of poverty and survival in a Cherokee town. A contrarian throughout his memoir, Lambert refuses to portray the Indian whose spiritual purity and commitment to community and cultural values carry the day. Instead, Lambert blames his parents for not supporting his education and holds other relatives accountable for their misdeeds. When his people oppose their casino on religious grounds, Lambert candidly declares that not Native American beliefs but Baptist religion leads the opposition. From end to end Lambert provides the truth of his Native world, no matter the disappointment of some readers.

The science fiction fantasy genre seems made for indigenous futurity. In *Field of Honor* (2004), Choctaw writer D. L. Birchfield imagines Choctaws have escaped settlers' rapine by building their own civilization—deep underground in southern Oklahoma. There Choctaws develop technologies to grow corn in immense greenhouses and to play their ancient game of stickball in vast stadiums. When social crisis threatens, Choctaw P. P. McDaniel, a Vietnam War veteran with Stockholm Cowardice Syndrome Dysfunction, emerges to save the day. In Cherokee writer Blake Hausman's *Riding the Trail of Tears* (2011), Georgians take a computer-simulated tour of the Cherokee removal. Novels imagining removal continue ironically to contribute to indigenous visions of futurity, as readers appear more and more comfortable returning to the atrocity. Some surmise that the Trail of Tears narrative offers struggles considered heroic by many North Americans, such as family separation and reunion, wagon trails west, and settling new lands. While Native Americans continue to recall such events with solemn resolve, in other minds they invite attractive, romantic longings. Perhaps only the futurist novel can break us free of them, as it seems to in *Riding the Trail of Tears*.

One day at the Trail of Tears virtual ride a group of anthropology students, sorority and fraternity members, and a Jewish family find themselves highjacked by ancient Cherokee wood nymphs, "little people" who have taken over the system and increased the programmed violence threshold. Though the participants die, one by one, at bayonet point on the way to stockades, they never even reach the trail west. Demanding Cherokee futurity, Hausman denies the desire of readers to experience the exodus. Instead, we discover that computerized Cherokees from different eras and walks of life have hidden within the computer program. These "Misfits" band together and plot to end the trail before it ever begins.

Like plains Indians of the frontier imagination, they descend on the cyber tourists and Cherokees slogging through the Cumberland Gap, but they soon find their ultimate enemy in the game's "stock Cherokees": "These stock Cherokees are scared and visibly trembling. They are professional victims...unaccustomed to sudden emancipation. Some tremble. Some whimper. Many want to flee. Deer Cooker, his face long and fallen, turns away from the Misfits." When the predictable victim Deer Cooker cannot bear the thought of freedom without a Trail of Tears, he bolts to warn others. Fish, a Misfit leader, takes action and "walks to the frontline of the Misfit collective, his obsidian crossbow luminous in the sun. He nonchalantly aims his weapon at Deer Cooker and shoots the tragic Cherokee in the back. Deer Cooker falls limply on the ground. The boy walks a few steps closer to the dying Indian and shoots him again, in the center of the head. Blood bubbles from Deer Cooker's body like water boiling over the edges of a full pot." In this daring passage, Hausman calls for the destruction of tragic Indian victims who, on the one hand, continue to colonize the minds of Native people and, on the other, serve the desires of those North American readers wishing to consume tragic Indians. For this author and for a growing number of Native American writers, that death promises a new indigenous person with, yes, futurity.

References

Preface

First Boy, "A Different Kind of Man," in *Native American Testimony: A Chronicle of Indian-White Relations from Prophesy to the Present, 1492–1992*, ed. Peter Nabokov (New York: Penguin, 1991), 27.

Chapter 1: The man made of words

N. Scott Momaday, "The Man Made of Words," in *The Remembered Earth: An Anthology of Contemporary Native American Literature*, ed. Geary Hobson (Albuquerque: University of New Mexico Press, 1979), 167, 168.

N. Scott Momaday, *House Made of Dawn* (1968; repr., New York: Perennial, 1989), 212.

William Apess, "Eulogy on King Philip, as Pronounced at the Odeon, in Federal Street, Boston" (1836), in *A Son of the Forest and Other Writings*, ed. Barry O'Connell (Amherst: University of Massachusetts Press, 1997), 114.

Chapter 2: Oral literatures

Washington Matthews, "The Night Chant," MAMNH 6 (1902): 142.

Larry Evers and Felipe S. Molina, *Yaqui Deer Songs* (Tucson: University of Arizona Press, 1987), 104.

John R. Swanton, *Tlingit Myths and Texts* (Washington, DC: Smithsonian Institution Bureau of American Ethnology, 1909), 395.

Chapter 3: To write in English

Samson Occom, "A Sermon, Preached at the Execution of Moses Paul, an Indian" (1899), in *Samson Occom and the Christian Indians of New England*, ed. W. DeLoss Love (Syracuse, NY: Syracuse University Press, 2000), 171.

Joseph Johnson, "Speech to the Oneidas" (1774), in *To Do Good to My Indian Brethren: The Writings of Joseph Johnson, 1751–1776*, ed. Laura J. Murray (Amherst: University of Massachusetts Press, 1998), 207.

William Apess, "An Indian's Looking-Glass for the White Man" (1833), in *A Son of the Forest and Other Writings*, ed. Barry O'Connell (Amherst: University of Massachusetts Press, 1997), 97.

William Apess, "A Son of the Forest" (1831), in *A Son of the Forest and Other Writings*, ed. Barry O'Connell (Amherst: University of Massachusetts Press, 1997), 4.

David Cusick, *Sketches of Ancient History of the Six Nations*, 3rd. ed. (Lockport, NY: Tuner and McCollum, Printers, Democrat Office, 1848), preface, 16.

Maris Bryant Pierce, *Address on the Present Condition and Prospects of the Aboriginal Inhabitants of North America, with Particular Reference to the Seneca Nation* (Philadelphia: J. Richards, 1839), reprinted in *American Indian Nonfiction: An Anthology of Writings, 1760s–1930s*, ed. Bernd C. Peyer (Norman: University of Oklahoma Press, 2007), 88.

Nathaniel Thayer Strong, "Appeal to the Christian Community on the Condition and Prospects of the New York Indians" (1841), in *American Indian Nonfiction: An Anthology of Writings, 1760s–1930s*, ed. Bernd C. Peyer (Norman: University of Oklahoma Press, 2007), 101.

Althea Bass, *Cherokee Messenger* (1936; repr., Norman: University of Oklahoma Press, 1996), 31.

Stan Hoig, *Sequoyah: The Cherokee Genius* (Oklahoma City: Oklahoma Historical Society, 1995), 32, 53–54.

Elias Boudinot, "To the Public, February 21, 1828," *Cherokee Phoenix*, in *Cherokee Editor: The Writings of Elias Boudinot*, ed. Theda Perdue (Athens: University of Georgia Press, 1996), 95.

Thurman Wilkins, *Cherokee Tragedy: The Ridge Family and the Decimation of a People* (Norman: University of Oklahoma, 1986), 203.

John Ridge, *Cherokee Phoenix*, February 18, 1832, p. 1, cols. 3–5.

Andrew Jackson, quoted by John Ridge to Elias Boudinot, *Cherokee Phoenix*, May 17, 1831, May 21, 1831, p. 2, col. 5; p. 3, cols. 1–2.

Lewis Cass, "Review of Documents and Proceedings Relating to the Formation and Progress of a Board in the City of New York, for the Emigration Preservation, and Improvement of the Aborigines of America," *North American Review* 30, no. 66 (January 1830): 67.

Timothy Sweet, "Cherokee 'Improvements' and the Removal Debate," in *American Georgics: Economy and Environment in Early American Literature* (Philadelphia: University of Pennsylvania Press, 2002), 122–152.

Elias Boudinot, "An Address to the Whites," (Philadelphia: William F. Geddes, 1826), reprinted in *Cherokee Editor: The Writings of Elias Boudinot*, ed. Theda Perdue (Athens: University of Georgia Press, 1996), 71, 74–75.

Sally M. Reece, "Letter to Reverend Daniel Campbell, July 25, 1828," quoted in *The Cherokee Removal: A Brief History with Documents*, eds. Theda Perdue and Michael D. Green (Boston: Bedford, 1995), 46–47.

William G. McLoughlin, *Cherokees and Missionaries, 1789–1839* (Norman: University of Oklahoma Press, 1995), 96.

Elias Boudinot, "Indian Clans, February 18, 1829," *Cherokee Phoenix*, in *Cherokee Editor: The Writings of Elias Boudinot*, ed. Theda Perdue (Athens: University of Georgia Press, 1996), 107.

Lewis Cass, "Review of Documents and Proceedings Relating to the Formation and Progress of a Board in the City of New York, for the Emigration Preservation, and Improvement of the Aborigines of America," *North American Review* 30, no. 66 (January 1830): 74.

Elias Boudinot, "An Address to the Whites," (Philadelphia: William F. Geddes, 1826), reprinted in *Cherokee Editor: The Writings of Elias Boudinot*, ed. Theda Perdue (Athens: University of Georgia Press, 1996), 68–69.

John Ridge, "Indian Address," *Religious Remembrancer* 10, no. 18 (December 15, 1822): 70, reprinted in *American Indian Nonfiction: An Anthology of Writings, 1760s–1930s*, ed. Bernd C. Peyer (Norman: University of Oklahoma Press, 2007), 119.

Chapter 4: From artifact to intellectual

Antoine LeClaire, "Certification" (1955), in *Black Hawk: An Autobiography*, ed. Donald Jackson (Urbana: University of Illinois Press, 1990), 35.

John B. Patterson, "Advertisement" (1955), in *Black Hawk: An Autobiography*, ed. Donald Jackson (Urbana: University of Illinois Press, 1990), 38.

Black Hawk, (1955) in *Black Hawk: An Autobiography*, ed. Donald Jackson (Urbana: University of Illinois Press, 1990), 89, 101.

Peter Jones, *History of the Ojibway Indians; with especial reference to their conversion to Christianity* (London: A. W. Bennett, 1860), 29.

Maureen Konkle, *Writing Indian Nations: Native Intellectuals and the Politics of Historiography, 1827–1863* (Chapel Hill: University of North Carolina Press, 2004), 184.

George Copway (Kahgegagahbowh), *Life, Letters, and Speeches*, eds. A. LaVonne Brown Ruoff and Donald B. Smith (Lincoln: University of Nebraska Press, 1997), 165.

William Whipple Warren, *History of the Ojibway People* (1885; repr., St. Paul: Minnesota Historical Society, 1984), 24, 26.

Simon Pokagon, *The Red Man's Rebuke by Chief Pokagon (Pottawattamie Chief)*, reprinted as *The Red Man's Greeting*, Hartford, MI: C. H. Engle, 1893, reprinted in *Indian Nation: Native American Literature and Nineteenth-Century Nationalisms*, by Cheryl Walker (Durham, NC: Duke University Press, 1997), 211.

John G. Neihardt, *Black Elk Speaks: Being the Life Story of a Holy Man of the Oglala Sioux* (1932; repr., Lincoln: University of Nebraska Press, 1979), 1–2.

Frank Linderman, *Pretty Shield: Medicine Woman of the Crows* (1932; repr., Lincoln: University of Nebraska Press, 2003), 66, 67.

Luther Standing Bear, *My People the Sioux* (1928; repr., Lincoln: University of Nebraska Press, 1975), 137.

Luther Standing Bear, *Land of the Spotted Eagle* (1933; repr., Lincoln: University of Nebraska Press, 1978), 254, 190.

Paul Radin, *Crashing Thunder: The Autobiography of an American Indian* (1926; repr., Ann Arbor: University of Michigan Press, 1999), 26, xxii.

Alexander Posey, "Choonstootee's Letter," *Arrow*, October 5, 1895, reprinted in *The Fus Fixico Letters*, eds. Daniel F. Littlefield Jr. and Carol A. Petty Hunter (Lincoln: University of Nebraska Press, 1993), 28–29.

Will Rogers, quoted in *The Best of Will Rogers*, ed. Bryan B. Sterling (New York: Crown, 1979), 180.

Fayette McKenzie, "Circular Letter from F. A. McKenzie," September 15, 1909, SAI Papers.

Arthur C. Parker, "Progress for the Indian," *Southern Workman* 41 (November 1912): 628–35.

John Milton Oskison, "Making an Individual of the Indian," *Everybody's Magazine* 16 (June 1907): 723.

Carlos Montezuma, "Our Treatment of the Indians from the Standpoint of One of Them," *Saturday Evening Post* 170 (May 21, 1898): 11.

Chapter 5: Native American literary studies

Elizabeth Cook-Lynn, "Who Stole Native American Studies?" *Wicazo Sa Review* 12, no. 1 (1997): 9.

Charles A. Eastman, *Indian Boyhood* (1902; repr., Lincoln: University of Nebraska Press, 1991), 51.

Luther Standing Bear, *Land of the Spotted Eagle* (1933; repr., Lincoln: University of Nebraska Press, 1978), 27.

N. Scott Momaday, "The Man Made of Words," in *The Remembered Earth: An Anthology of Contemporary Native American Literature*, ed. Geary Hobson (Albuquerque: University of New Mexico Press, 1979), 168, 172, 164–65.

Paula Gunn Allen, "Iyani: It Goes This Way," in *The Remembered Earth: An Anthology of Contemporary Native American Literature*, ed. Geary Hobson (Albuquerque: University of New Mexico Press, 1979), 191.

Paula Gunn Allen, "This Wilderness in My Blood: Spiritual Foundations of the Poetry of Five American Indian Women," in *The Sacred Hoop: Recovering the Feminine in American Indian Traditions* (1986; repr., Boston: Beacon, 1992), 165.

Louis Owens, *Other Destinies: Understanding the American Indian Novel* (Norman: University of Oklahoma Press, 1992), 22, 26.

Robert Allen Warrior, *Tribal Secrets: Recovering American Indian Intellectual Traditions* (Minneapolis: University of Minnesota, 1995), xvi, 2.

Craig S. Womack, *Red on Red: Native American Literary Separatism* (Minneapolis: University of Minnesota Press, 1999), 4–7.

Shari Huhndorf, *Mapping the Americas* (Ithaca, NY: Cornell University Press, 2009), 2–4.

Vizenor, Gerald, *Word Arrows: Indians and Whites in the New Fur Trade* (Minneapolis: University of Minnesota Press, 1978), 3–4.

James Welch, *Winter in the Blood* (1974; repr., New York: Penguin, 1986), 174.

Leslie Marmon Silko, *Yellow Woman and a Beauty of the Spirit: Essays on Native American Life Today* (New York: Simon and Schuster, 1996), 32.

Simon J. Ortiz, "Towards a National Indian Literature: Cultural Authenticity in Nationalism," *MELUS* 8, no. 2 (1981): 9, 10.

Simon J. Ortiz, "Song/Poetry and Language: Expression and Perception" (1983), in *Speak to Me Words*, eds. Dean Rader and Janice Gould (Tucson: University of Arizona Press, 2003), 246.

Chapter 6: The Native novel

John Rollin Ridge, *Joaquin Murieta, the Celebrated California Bandit* (1854; repr., Norman: University of Oklahoma Press, 1955), 87.

S. Alice Callahan, *Wynema, a Child of the Forest* (1891; repr., Lincoln: University of Nebraska Press, 1997), 45.

John Milton Oskison, *The Singing Bird: A Cherokee Novel* (Norman: University of Oklahoma Press, 2007 [c. 1930s]), 149.

D'Arcy McNickle, *The Surrounded* (1936; repr., Albuquerque: University of New Mexico Press, 1994), 62.

Sherman Alexie, *Reservation Blues* (New York: Grove Press, 1995), 7.

Irvin Morris, *From the Glittering World: A Navajo Story* (Norman: University of Oklahoma Press, 1997), 33, 124, 189.

Greg Sarris, *Grand Avenue: A Novel in Stories* (New York: Penguin, 1994), 211.

Janet Campbell Hale, *The Jailing of Cecelia Capture* (1985; repr., Albuquerque: University of New Mexico Press, 2000), 7.

Craig S. Womack, *Drowning in Fire* (Tucson: University of Arizona Press, 2001), 104.

Leslie Marmon Silko, *Almanac of the Dead* (New York: Simon and Schuster, 1991), 19.

Gerald Vizenor, *Bearheart: The Heirship Chronicles* (1978; repr., Minneapolis: University of Minnesota Press, 1990), 145.

Chapter 7: Indigenous futurity

Clyde Warrior, "The War on Poverty" (1973), in *Great Documents in American Indian History*, ed. Wayne Moquin (New York: Da Capo Press, 1995), 357.

Simon J. Ortiz, "A Story of How a Wall Stands," *Going for the Rain* (New York: Harper and Row, 1976), reprinted in *Woven Stone* (Tucson: University of Arizona Press, 1992), 145.

Louis Little Coon Oliver, "Empty Kettle," in *Harper's Anthology of Twentieth-Century Native American Poetry*, ed. Duane Niatum (New York: Harper, 1988), 5.

James Welch, "The Man from Washington" (1971), in *Riding the Earthboy 40* (Pittsburgh: Carnegie Mellon University Press, 1997), 35.

Simon J. Ortiz, *From Sand Creek* (Tucson: University of Arizona Press, 1981), 75, 9.

Louise Erdrich, "Indian Boarding School: The Runaways," in *Harper's Anthology of Twentieth-Century Native American Poetry*, ed. Duane Niatum (New York: Harper, 1988), 334.

Joy Harjo, *A Map to the Next World* (New York: W. W. Norton, 2000), 16, 102.

Eric Gansworth, *Nickel Eclipse* (East Lansing: Michigan State University Press, 2000), 170–71.

Mark Turcotte, "No Pie," in *Exploding Chippewas* (Evanston, IL: Northwestern University Press, 2002), 51.

Lynn Riggs, *The Cherokee Night*, in *The Cherokee Night and Other Plays* (1932; repr., Norman: University of Oklahoma Press, 2003), 151.

Richard Van Camp, *The Lesser Blessed* (Vancouver: Douglas and McIntyre, 1996), 8.

Tiffany Midge, *Outlaws, Renegades, and Saints: A Diary of a Mixed-Up Halfbreed* (Greenfield Center, NY: Greenfield Review, 1996), 102.

Eric Gansworth, *Breathing the Monster Alive* (Treadwell, NY: Bright Hill Press, 2006), 31.

Blake Hausman, *Riding the Trail of Tears* (Lincoln: University of Nebraska Press, 2011), 270, 271.

Further reading

Literature

Alexie, Sherman. *Indian Killer*. New York: Atlantic Monthly, 1996.

Alexie, Sherman. *Reservation Blues*. New York: Grove Press, 1995.

Allen, Paula Gunn. "Iyani: It Goes This Way." In *The Remembered Earth: An Anthology of Contemporary Native American Literature*. Edited by Geary Hobson, 191–193. Albuquerque: University of New Mexico Press, 1979.

Allen, Paula Gunn. *The Woman Who Owned the Shadows*. San Francisco: Spinters, 1983.

Apess, William. *Eulogy on King Philip, as Pronounced at the Odeon, in Federal Street, Boston*. Boston: By the author, 1836. In *A Son of the Forest and Other Writings*. Edited by Barry O'Connell, 105–138. Amherst: University of Massachusetts Press, 1997.

Apess, William. *The Experiences of Five Christian Indians of the Pequot Tribe*. Boston: By the author, 1833. In *A Son of the Forest and Other Writings*. Edited by Barry O'Connell, 3–56. Amherst: University of Massachusetts Press, 1997.

Apess, William. "An Indian's Looking Glass for the White Man." In *The Experiences of Five Christian Indians of the Pequot Tribe*. Boston: By the author, 1833. In *A Son of the Forest and Other Writings*. Edited by Barry O'Connell, 95–101. Amherst: University of Massachusetts Press, 1997.

Apess, William. *Nullification of the Unconstitutional Laws of Massachusetts Relative to the Marshpee Tribe; or, The Pretended Riot Explained*. Boston: Jonathan Howe, 1835. In *On Our Own Ground: The Complete Writings of William Apess, A Pequot*.

Edited by Barry O'Connell, 166–274. Amherst: University of Massachusetts Press, 1992.

Apess, William. *A Son of the Forest: The Experience of William Apes, a Native of the Forest, Comprising a Notice of the Pequot Tribe of Indians*. New York: By the author, 1829. In *A Son of the Forest and Other Writings*. Edited by Barry O'Connell, 3–56. Amherst: University of Massachusetts Press, 1997.

Armstrong, Jeannette C. *Slash*. Penticton, BC: Theytus Books, 1985.

Aupaumut, Hendrick. "History of the Muh-he-con-nuk Indians, ca. 1790." In *Stockbridge, Past and Present; or Records of an Old Mission Station*. Edited by Electa Jones, 15–23. Springfield, MA: Samuel Bowles and Company, 1854.

Bell, Betty Louise. *Faces in the Moon*. Norman: University of Oklahoma Press, 1994.

Birchfield, D. L. *Field of Honor*. Norman: University of Oklahoma Press, 2004.

Blackbird, Andrew Jackson. *The Indian Problem, from the Indian's Standpoint*. Philadelphia: National Indian Association, 1900. In *American Indian Nonfiction: An Anthology of Writings, 1760s–1930s*. Edited by Bernd C. Peyer, 244–252. Norman: University of Oklahoma Press, 2007.

Black Hawk. *Life of Ma-ka-tai-me-she-kia-kiak, or Black Hawk*. Edited by J. B. Patterson. Cincinnati: Unidentified publisher, 1833. Reprint, *Black Hawk: An Autobiography*. Urbana: University of Illinois Press, 1955.

Boudinot, Elias Cornelius. "An Address to the Whites." Philadelphia: William F. Geddes, 1826. Reprint, *Cherokee Editor: The Writings of Elias Boudinot*. Edited by Theda Perdue, 244–252. Athens: University of Georgia Press, 1996.

Boudinot, Elias Cornelius. *Elias Cornelius Boudinot: A Life on the Cherokee Border*, James W. Parins. Norman: University of Oklahoma Press, 2006.

Brown, Catherine. *Memoir of Catherine Brown: A Christian Indian of the Cherokee Nation*. Edited by Rufus Anderson. Boston: Samuel T. Armstrong, and Crocker and Brewster, 1825.

Callahan, Alice. *Wynema a Child of the Forest*. Chicago: H. J. Smith and Company, 1891. Reprint, Lincoln: University of Nebraska Press, 1997.

Campbell, Maria. *Halfbreed*. Lincoln: University of Nebraska Press, 1978.

Coolidge, Sherman. "The Function of the Society of American Indians." *The Quarterly Journal of the Society of American Indians* 2.1 (January–March 1914): 186–190. In *American Indian*

Nonfiction: An Anthology of Writings, 1760s–1930s. Edited by
Bernd C. Peyer, 345–348. Norman: University of Oklahoma
Press, 2007.

Copway, George. *Life, Letters, and Speeches of Kah-ge-ga-gah-bowh.*
(Originally published as *The Life, History, and Travels of
Kah-ge-ga-gah-bowh (George Copway), a Young Indian Chief of the
Ojibwa Nation, A Convert to the Christian Faith, and a Missionary
to His People for Twelve Years,* 1847 [New York: S. W. Benedict,
1850].) Edited by LaVonne Brown Ruoff and Donald B. Smith.
Lincoln: University of Nebraska Press, 1997.

Copway, George. *Running Sketches of Men and Places, in England,
France, Germany, Belgium, and Scotland.* New York: J. C. Riker,
1851.

Cusick, David. *Sketches of Ancient History of the Six Nations.*
Lockport, NY: Turner and McCollum, Printers, Democrat Office,
1848.

Deloria, Ella. *Waterlily.* Reprint, Lincoln: University of Nebraska
Press, 1988.

Dembiki, Matt. *Trickster: Native American Tales, a Graphic
Collection.* Golden, CO: Fulcrum, 2010.

Downing, Todd. *The Cat Screams.* Reprint, Downing: New York:
Doubleday, Doran and Company, 1934.

Duncan, DeWitt Clinton. "A Momentous Occasion." *Indian Chieftain*
(Vinita, Cherokee Nation), June 24, 1897. Reprint, *Native
American Writing in the Southeast: An Anthology, 1875–1935.*
Edited by Daniel F. Littlefield Jr. and James W. Parins, 31–37.
Jackson: University Press of Mississippi, 1995.

Eastman, Charles. *From the Deep Woods to Civilization.* Reprint,
Boston: Little, Brown, and Co., 1916.

Eastman, Charles. *Indian Boyhood.* Reprint, Boston: Little, Brown,
and Co., 1902.

Erdrich, Louise. "Indian Boarding School: The Runaways." In *Harper's
Anthology of Twentieth-Century Native American Poetry.* Edited by
Duane Niatum, 334. New York: Harper, 1988.

Erdrich, Louise. *Love Medicine.* 1984. New York: Perennial, 1993.

Erdrich, Louise. *Tracks.* New York: Perennial, 1988.

Eubanks, William. "For Land in Severalty, and Statehood." *Cherokee
Advocate* (Tahlequah, Cherokee Nation), April 18, 1894. In *Native
American Writing in the Southeast: An Anthology, 1875–1935.*
Edited by Daniel F. Littlefield Jr. and James W. Parins, 26–27.
Jackson: University Press of Mississippi, 1995.

First Boy. "A Different Kind of Man." In *Native American Testimony: A Chronicle of Indian-White Relations from Prophesy to the Present, 1492–1992*. Edited by Peter Nabokov, 26–29. New York: Penguin, 1991.

Gansworth, Eric. *Breathing the Monster Alive*. Treadwell, NY: Bright Hill Press, 2006.

Gansworth, Eric. *Nickel Eclipse*. East Lansing: Michigan State University Press, 2000.

Gansworth, Eric. *Smoke Dancing*. East Lansing: Michigan State University Press, 2004.

Geiogamah, Hanay. *Body Indian. Seventh Generation: An Anthology of Native American Plays*. Edited by Mimi Gisolfi D'Aponte, 1–37. New York: Theatre Communications Group, 1972.

Geronimo. *Geronimo's Story of His Life: A Legendary Warrior and Shaman Recounts the Beliefs and Customs of His People in One of Native American History's Most Extraordinary Documents*. Edited by S. M. Barrett. New York: Duffield and Company, 1906.

Hale, Janet Campbell. *The Jailing of Cecelia Capture*. Albuquerque: University of New Mexico Press, 1985.

Harjo, Joy. *A Map to the Next World*. New York: W. W. Norton, 2000.

Hausman, Blake. *Riding the Trail of Tears*. Lincoln: University of Nebraska Press, 2011.

Hewitt, J. N. B. "The Teaching of Ethnology in Indian Schools." *The Quarterly Journal of the Society of American Indians* 1.1 (April 15, 1913): 30–35. In *American Indian Nonfiction: An Anthology of Writings, 1760s–1930s*. Edited by Bernd Peyer, 328–332. Norman: University of Oklahoma Press, 2007.

Highway, Tomson. *Dry Lips Oughta Move to Kapuskasing*. Toronto: Fifth House Publishers, 1989.

Highway, Tomson. *Rez Sisters*. Toronto: Fifth House Publishers, 1986.

Hill, Roberta. nee Roberta Hill Whiteman. *Star Quilt*. Duluth, MN: Holy Cow! Press, 2001.

Hogan, Linda. *Mean Spirit*. New York: Ivy Books, 1990.

Hogan, Linda. *Power*. New York: W. W. Norton, 1999.

Howe, LeAnne. *Shell Shaker*. San Francisco: Aunt Lute Books, 2001.

Johnson, E. Pauline. *Flint and Feather (Collected Verse)*. New York: Hodder and Stoughton, 1917.

Johnson, Joseph. "Speech to the Oneidas." 1774. Reprint, *To Do Good to My Indian Brethren: The Writings of Joseph Johnson, 1751–1776*.

Edited by Laura J. Murray. Amherst: University of Massachusetts Press, 1998.

Jones, Peter. *History of the Ojibway Indians; with Especial Reference to Their Conversion to Christianity*. London: A. W. Bennett, 1860.

King, Thomas. *Green Grass, Running Water*. New York: Bantam, 1993.

King, Thomas. *Truth and Bright Water*. New York: Grove, 1999.

La Flesche, Francis. *The Middle Five: Indian Schoolboys of the Omaha Tribe*. Reprint, Lincoln: University of Nebraska Press, 1978.

Lambert, Leonard. *Up From These Hills*. Lincoln: University of Nebraska Press, 2011.

Linderman, Frank. *Plenty Coup: Chief of the Crows*. (Originally published as *American: The Life Story of a Great Indian, Plenty-coup, Chief of the Crows* [New York: John Day Company, 1930].) Lincoln: University of Nebraska Press, 1962.

Linderman, Frank. *Pretty Shield: Medicine Woman of Crows*. (Originally published as *Red Mother* [New York: John Day Company, 1932].) Lincoln: University of Nebraska Press, 2003.

Lurie, Nancy Oestreich. *Mountain Wolf Woman, Sister of Crashing Thunder: The Autobiography of a Winnebago Indian*. Ann Arbor: University of Michigan Press, 1961.

Maracle, Lee. *Ravensong*. Vancouver, BC: Press Gang, 1993.

Mathews, John Joseph. *Sundown*. New York: Longman, Green, 1934.

Maungwudaus. *An Account of the Chippewa Indians: Who Have Been Travelling among the Whites*. Boston: By the author, 1848.

McNickle, D'Arcy. *Runner in the Sun: A Story of Indian Maize*. Reprint, New York: Holt, Rinehart, and Winston, 1954.

McNickle, D'Arcy. *The Surrounded*. Reprint, New York: Dodd, Mead, 1936.

McNickle, D'Arcy. *Wind from an Enemy Sky*. Reprint, New York: Harper and Row, 1978.

Midge, Tiffany. *Outlaws, Renegades, and Saints*. Greenfield Center, NY: Greenfield Review, 1996.

Mojica, Monique. *Princess Pocahontas and the Blue Spots*. Toronto: Three O'Clock Press, 1991.

Momaday, N. Scott. *House Made of Dawn*. New York: Harper and Row, 1968.

Momaday, N. Scott. "The Man Made of Words." In *The Remembered Earth: An Anthology of Contemporary Native American Literature*.

Edited by Geary Hobson, 162–173. Albuquerque: University of New Mexico Press, 1979.

Momaday, N. Scott. *The Way to Rainy Mountain*. Albuquerque: University of New Mexico Press, 1969.

Montezuma, Carlos. "Our Treatment of the Indians from the Standpoint of One of Them." *Saturday Evening Post* 170 (May 21, 1898): 11–12.

Morris, Irvin. *From the Glittering World*. Norman: University of Oklahoma Press, 2000.

Moses, Daniel David. *Almighty Voice and His Wife*. Toronto: Playwrights Canada Press, 2010.

Mourning Dove. *Cogewea, the Half-Blood*. Reprint, Boston: Four Seas Co., 1927.

Neihardt, John G. *Black Elk Speaks: Being the Life Story of a Holy Man of the Oglala Sioux*. Reprint, New York: William Morrow and Co., 1932.

Occom, Samson. *Sermon Preached at the Execution of Moses Paul, and Indian*. New Haven, CT: Press of Thomas and Samuel Green, 1899. Reprint, *Samson Occom and the Christian Indians of New England.* Edited by W. DeLoss Love. Syracuse, NY: Syracuse University Press, 1772.

Oliver, Louis Little Coon. "Empty Kettle." In *Harper's Anthology of Twentieth-Century Native American Poetry*. Edited by Duane Niatum. New York: Harper, 1988.

Ortiz, Simon. *From Sand Creek*. Tucson: University of Arizona Press, 1981.

Ortiz, Simon. "Song/Poetry and Language—Expression and Perception." *Symposium of the Whole*. Berkeley: University of California Press, 1978. Reprint, *Speak to Me Words*. Edited by Dean Rader and Janice Gould, 235–246. Tucson: University of Arizona Press, 1993.

Ortiz, Simon. "A Story of How a Wall Stands." In *Going for the Rain*. New York: Harper and Row, 1976. Reprint, *Woven Stone*. Edited by Simon Ortiz, 145. Tucson: University of Arizona Press, 1992.

Oskison, John Milton. *Black Jack Davy*. New York: Appleton, 1926.

Oskison, John Milton. *Brothers Three*. New York: Macmillan, 1935.

Oskison, John Milton. *The Singing Bird: A Cherokee Novel*. Reprint, Norman: University of Oklahoma, 2007.

Oskison, John Milton. *Wild Harvest: A Novel of Transition Days in Oklahoma*. New York: Appleton, 1925.

Parker, Arthur C. *The Code of Handsome Lake*. New York: New York State Museum Bulletin, 1913.

Parker, Arthur C. *The Constitution of the Five Nations*. New York: New York State Museum Bulletin, 1916.

Pierce, Maris Bryant. *Address on the Present Condition and Prospects of the Aboriginal Inhabitants of North America, with Particular Reference to the Seneca Nation*. Philadelphia: J. Richards, 1839. In *American Indian Nonfiction: An Anthology of Writings, 1760s–1930s*. Edited by Bernd C. Peyer, 87–95. Norman: University of Oklahoma Press, 2007.

Pokagon, Simon. *The Red Man's Rebuke by Chief Pokagon (Pottawattamie Chief)*. Reprinted as *The Red Man's Greeting*, Hartford, MI: C. H. Engle, 1893. Reprint, *Indian Nation: Native American Literature and Nineteenth-Century Nationalisms*, by Cheryl Walker, 211–220. Durham, NC: Duke University Press, 1997.

Pomplun, Tom. *Native American Classics*. Mount Horeb, WI: Eureka, 2013.

Posey, Alexander. "Choonstootee's Letter." *Arrow*, October 5, 1895. Reprint, *The Fus Fixico Letters*. Edited by Daniel F. Littlefield Jr. and Carol A. Petty Hunter, 28–29. Lincoln: University of Nebraska Press, 1993.

Power, Susan. *Grass Dancer*. G. P. Putnam's Sons, 1994.

Prewett, Frank James. "The Red-Man." In *Harper's Anthology of Twentieth-Century Native American Poetry*. Edited by Duane Niatum. New York: Harper, 1988.

Radin, Paul. *Crashing Thunder: The Autobiography of an American Indian*. Reprint, D. Appleton and Co., 1926.

Red Jacket. 1805. "You have got our country, but are not satisfied; you want to force religion upon us." In *Lives of Famous Indian Chiefs*. Edited by Norman B. Wood, 254–256. Aurora, IL: American Indian Historical Publishing Company, 1906. Reprint, *Great Speeches by Native Americans*. Edited by Bob Blaisdell, 41–43. New York: Dover, 2000.

Reese, Sally M. "Letter to Reverend Daniel Campbell, July 25, 1828." Quoted in *The Cherokee Removal: A Brief History with Documents*. Edited by Theda Perdue and Michael D. Green, 46–47. Boston: Bedford, 1995.

Ridge, John. "Indian Address." *Religious Remembrancer* 10.18 (December 15, 1822): 70. In *American Indian Nonfiction: An*

Anthology of Writings, 1760s–1930s. Edited by Bernd C. Peyer, 119–121. Norman: University of Oklahoma Press, 2007.

Ridge, John. "Letter." *Cherokee Phoenix*, February 18, 1832, p. 1, cols. 3–5.

Ridge, John Rollin. *Life and Adventures of Joaquin Murieta, the Celebrated California Bandit*. Reprint, San Francisco: W. R. Cook and Co., 1854.

Riggs, Lynn. 1932. "The Cherokee Night." In *The Cherokee Night and Other Plays*. Edited by Lynn Riggs, 106–211. Reprint, Norman: University of Oklahoma Press, 2003.

Riggs, Lynn. 1931. "Green Grow the Lilacs." In *The Cherokee Night and Other Plays*. Edited by Lynn Riggs, 2–105. Reprint, Norman: University of Oklahoma Press, 2003.

Robinson, Eden. *Monkey Beach*. Boston: Houghton Mifflin, 2000.

Rogers, Will. *The Best of Will Rogers*. Edited by Bryan B. Sterling. New York: Crown, 1979.

Ross, John. *The Papers of Chief John Ross*. 2 vols. Edited by Gary E. Moulton. Norman: University of Oklahoma Press, 1984.

Sarris, Greg. *Grand Avenue*. Reprint, New York: Hyperion, 1994.

Sarris, Greg. *Watermelon Nights*. Reprint, New York: Hyperion, 1998.

Schoolcraft, Jane Johnston. "The Forsaken Brother: A Chippewa Tale." In *Native American Women's Writing, c. 1800–1924: An Anthology*. Edited by Karen L. Kilcup, 67–69. Oxford: Blackwell, 2000.

Silko, Leslie Marmon. *Almanac of the Dead*. New York: Simon and Schuster, 1991.

Silko, Leslie Marmon. *Ceremony*. New York: Penguin, 1977.

Spiderwoman Theater. "*Winnetou's Snake Oil Show from Wigwam City.*" *Canadian Theatre Review* 68 (Fall 1991): 56–63.

Standing Bear, Luther. *Land of the Spotted Eagle*. Reprint, New York: Houghton Mifflin, 1933.

Standing Bear, Luther. *My People the Sioux*. Reprint, New York: Houghton Mifflin, 1928.

Strong, Nathaniel Thayer. *Appeal to the Christian Community on the Condition and Prospects of the New York Indians*. Buffalo: Press of Thomas and Company, 1841. In *American Indian Nonfiction: An Anthology of Writings, 1760s–1930s*. Edited by Bernd C. Peyer, 100–107. Norman: University of Oklahoma Press, 2007.

Taylor, Drew Hayden. *Only Drunks and Children Tell the Truth: Seventh Generation; An Anthology of Native American Plays.* Edited by Mimi Gisolfi D'Aponte, 201–265. New York: Theatre Communications Group, 1999.

Tohe, Laura. *No Parole Today.* Albuquerque: West End Press, 1999.

Treuer, David. *The Hiawatha.* Reprint, New York: Picador, 2000.

Turcotte, Mark. "No Pie." In *Exploding Chippewas.* Edited by Mark Turcotte, 51. Evanston, IL: Northwestern University Press, 2002.

Van Camp, Richard. *The Lesser Blessed.* Vancouver, BC: Douglas and McIntyre, 1996.

Vizenor, Gerald. *Bearheart: The Heirship Chronicles.* (Originally published as *St. Paul: Truck Press, 1978.*) Minneapolis: University of Minnesota Press, 1990.

Vizenor, Gerald. *The Heirs of Columbus.* Middletown, CT: Wesleyan University Press, 1991.

Vizenor, Gerald. *Interior Landscapes: Autobiographical Myths and Metaphors.* Minneapolis: University of Minnesota Press, 1990.

Vizenor, Gerald. *Word Arrows: Indians and Whites in the New Fur Trade.* Minneapolis: University of Minnesota Press, 1978.

Wagamese, Richard. *Keeper 'n Me.* Toronto: Doubleday, 1994.

Warren, William Whipple. *History of the Ojibway People.* Saint Paul: Minnesota Historical Society, 1885. Reprint, St. Paul: Minnesota Historical Society, 1984.

Warrior, Clyde. "The War on Poverty." In *Rural Poverty.* Edited by Clyde Warrior, 143–147. Washington, DC: federal report, 1967. Reprint, *Great Documents in American Indian History.* Edited by Wayne Moquin, 355–357. New York: Da Capo Press, 1995.

Welch, James. *The Death of Jim Loney.* New York: Penguin, 1979.

Welch, James. *Fools Crow.* New York: Penguin, 1986.

Welch, James. *The Heartsong of Charging Elk.* New York: Doubleday, 2000.

Welch, James. *The Indian Lawyer.* Reprint, New York: W. W. Norton and Co., 1990.

Welch, James. "The Man from Washington." In *Riding the Earthboy 40.* Edited by James Welch, 35. Reprint, Cleveland: World Publishing Co., 1971.

Welch, James. *Winter in the Blood.* Reprint, New York: Harper and Row, 1974.

Winnemucca Hopkins, Sarah. *Life among the Piutes: Their Wrongs and Claims.* New York: G. P. Putnam Sons, 1883. Reprint, Reno: University of Nevada Press, 1994.

Womack, Craig. *Drowning in Fire.* Tucson: University of Arizona Press, 2001.

Yellow Robe, William S. Jr. *The Independence of Eddie Rose: Seventh Generation; An Anthology of Native American Plays.* Edited by Mimi Gisolfi D'Aponte, 39–97. New York: Theatre Communications Group, 1999.

Young Bear, Ray. *Remnants of the First Earth.* New York: Grove, 1996.

Zitkala-Ša. "The Soft-Hearted Sioux." In *American Indian Stories,* 48–55. Washington, DC: Hayworth Publishing House, 1921. Reprint, Mineola, NY: Dover, 2009.

Contents

Edmunds, R. David, Frederick E. Hoxie, and Neal Salisbury. *The People: A History of Native America.* Boston: Houghton Mifflin, 2007.

Pearce, Roy Harvey. *The Savages of America: A Study of the Indian and the Idea of Civilization.* Baltimore: Johns Hopkins University Press, 1953. Reprinted with foreword by Arnold Krupat. *Savagism and Civilization: A Study of the Indian and the American Mind.* Berkeley: University of California Press, 1988.

Warrior, Robert, ed. *The World of Indigenous North America.* London: Routledge, 2014.

Wilkins, David E., and K. Tsianina Lomawaima. *Uneven Ground: American Indian Sovereignty and Federal Law.* Norman: University of Oklahoma Press, 2001.

Wilkinson, Charles F. *Blood Struggle: The Rise of Modern Indian Nations.* New York: W.W. Norton, 2006.

Oral tradition

Kroeber, Karl. *Artistry in Native American Myths.* Lincoln: University of Nebraska Press, 1998.

Krupat, Arnold. *"That the People Might Live": Loss and Renewal in the Native American Elegy.* Ithaca, NY: Cornell University Press, 2012.

Ramsey, Jarold. *Reading the Fire: The Traditional Indian Literatures of America*. Seattle: University of Washington Press, 1999.

Ruoff, A. LaVonne Brown. "The Survival of Tradition: American Indian Oral and Written Narratives." *Massachusetts Review* 27.2 (1986): 274–293.

Silko, Leslie Marmon. "Interior and Exterior Landscapes: The Pueblo Migration Stories." In *Yellow Woman and a Beauty of the Spirit: Essays on Native American Life Today*. Edited by Leslie Marmon Silko, 25–47. New York: Simon and Schuster, 1996.

Early writing

Konkle, Maureen. *Writing Indian Nations: Native Intellectuals and the Politics of Historiography, 1827–1863*. Chapel Hill: University of North Carolina Press, 2004.

O'Brien, Jean M. *Firsting and Lasting: Writing Indians Out of Existence in New England*. Minneapolis: University of Minnesota Press, 2010.

Perdue, Theda, and Michael Green. *The Cherokee Nation and the Trail of Tears*. New York: Penguin, 2008.

Peyer, Bernd. *The Tutor'd Mind: Indian Missionary-Writers in Antebellum America*. Amherst: University of Massachusetts Press, 1997.

Wyss, Hilary E. *Writing Indians: Literacy, Christianity, and Native Community in Early America*. Amherst: University of Massachusetts Press, 2000.

Resistance and assimilation

Calloway, Colin G. *One Vast Winter Count: The Native American West before Lewis and Clark*. Lincoln: University of Nebraska Press, 2003.

Hoxie, Frederick E. *A Final Promise: The Campaign to Assimilate the Indians, 1880–1920*. Lincoln: University of Nebraska Press, 2001.

Jung, Patrick J. *The Black Hawk War of 1832*. Norman: University of Oklahoma Press, 2007.

Kelman, Ari. *A Misplaced Massacre: Struggling over the Memory of Sand Creek*. Cambridge, MA: Harvard University Press, 2013.

Maddox, Lucy. *Citizen Indians: Native American Intellectuals, Race, and Reform*. Ithaca, NY: Cornell University Press, 2005.

Studying Native Americans

Elliott, Michael A. *The Culture Concept: Writing and Difference in the Age of Realism*. Minneapolis: University of Minnesota Press, 2002.

Huhndorf, Shari. *Mapping the Americas: The Transnational Politics of Contemporary Native Culture*. Ithaca, NY: Cornell University Press, 2009.

Krupat, Arnold. *Red Matters: Native American Studies*. Philadelphia: University of Pennsylvania Press, 2002.

Smith, Paul Chaat, and Robert Allen Warrior. *Like a Hurricane: The Indian Movement from Alcatraz to Wounded Knee*. New York: New Press, 1997.

Vizenor, Gerald. *Fugitive Poses: Native American Indian Scenes of Absence and Presence*. Minneapolis: University of Minnesota Press, 2000.

Weaver, Jace, Craig S. Womack, and Robert Warrior. *American Indian Literary Nationalism*. Albuquerque: University of New Mexico Press, 2005.

The novel

Bevis, William W. "Native American Novels: Homing In." In *Recovering the Word: Essays on Native American Literature*. Edited by Brian Swann and Arnold Krupat, 580–620. Berkeley: University of California Press, 1987.

Fixico, Donald L. *Termination and Relocation: Federal Indian Policy, 1945–1960*. Albuquerque: University of New Mexico Press, 1986.

Owens, Louis. *Other Destinies: Understanding the American Indian Novel*. Norman: University of Oklahoma Press, 1992.

Teuton, Sean. *Red Land, Red Power: Grounding Knowledge in the American Indian Novel*. Durham, NC: Duke University Press, 2008.

Wilson, Michael D. *Writing Home: Indigenous Narratives of Resistance*. East Lansing: Michigan State University Press, 2008.

Looking ahead

Clifford, James. *Returns: Becoming Indigenous in the Twenty-First Century*. Cambridge, MA: Harvard University Press, 2013.

Deloria, Philip J. *Indians in Unexpected Places*. Lawrence: University of Kansas Press, 2004.

Lyons, Scott Richard. *X-Marks: Native Signatures of Assent*. Minneapolis: University of Minnesota Press, 2010.

Smith, Paul Chaat. *Everything You Know about Indians Is Wrong*. Minneapolis: University of Minnesota Press, 2009.

Index